TELEVISIONS

TELEVISIONS

One Season in American Television

MARC ELIOT

St. Martin's Press
New York

Library of Congress Cataloging in Publication Data

Eliot, Marc.
    Televisions, one season of American television.

    1. Television broadcasting—United States.
2. Television programs—United States—Rating.
I. Title.
PN1992.3.U5E383   1983   384.55'4'0973   82–17015
ISBN 0–312–79076–7

Design by Kingsley Parker

First Edition

10 9 8 7 6 5 4 3 2 1

This book is dedicated to the memory of Al Hodge—
America's first man in space.

Contents

TELEVISIONS

Prologue

Scattered among the thirty-six American television seasons to date are a handful that, for one reason or another, are outstanding. It might have been a season with a program or a series that dominated all other programming for that year and perhaps many that followed. The year 1947 gave America Milton Berle, who, in the role of "Mr. Television," is often credited with selling enough television sets to turn a novelty into an ongoing form of entertainment. The classic thirty-nine episodes of "The Honeymooners" appeared in 1956, elevating and refining the art of situation comedy. In 1952 Jack Webb produced and starred in the iconographic "Dragnet," introducing a style of television drama still popular today: quick cuts, heavy theme music, close-ups, cliff-hangers. The year 1962 brought an end to the urbane Jack Paar and the beginning of the rural, lovable Johnny Carson on "The Tonight Show"; 1971 changed the collective sit-com smile to a cynical smirk with "All In The Family"; and 1977 gave America "Roots."

Other seasons are remembered for events outside the

1

medium, which television, through its immediacy and sense of drama, was able to bring into our living rooms and our consciences. The televised Army-McCarthy hearings dominated 1953. The 1963 assassination of John F. Kennedy brought four days of unforgettable political and social terror and trauma. The moon landing was broadcast in 1969. In 1974 the locale shifted to Watergate. The death of pop culture's innocence was broadcast in 1980 as the children of the sixties wept in New York's Central Park for John Lennon. Television was there in 1981 when President Reagan was wounded and when the Pope was gunned down a few weeks later.

The 1981–1982 television season was dominated by off-screen, unscheduled events and issues—political, social, economic. Politically, there were continuing strikes that threatened to bring the entire entertainment industry to a halt. Socially, there was the rise of Jerry Falwell's Moral Majority, reminiscent of the fifties' era of blacklisting and McCarthyism. Economically, there was the explosion of the cable systems, the first viable alternative to the broadcasting monopoly of the three networks since the beginning of commercial television.

Of course, these three dominating issues were interchangeable in their influence and structure: politics was certainly to play a part in the rise of the Moral Majority, one or more of its principals surely being groomed for political office. The angry, bitter strikes of Hollywood in the eighties were as much a social phenomenon as they were political protest, and the cable revolution was exactly that—a revolution threatening to remove the social domination of a single style of broadcasting from the hands of the corporate few in favor of a more specialized if less privileged group of viewers.

Television, already lower-cased by middle-brow critics seeking to high-brow themselves by downgrading the medium, could hardly be expected to take issue with the issues. Television, they tell us, is best trashed by its own trash. Television, they say, causes violence, good reason never to turn it on. In reality, Television doesn't preach violence, it promotes passivity. The very act of watching television (the average American is up to six and a half hours a day) is its own very passive proof. The nature of television's structure—the aggressive plane flying the passive pilot—makes the medium so prone to attack. It's not that far a leap to go from critical outcry to moral outrage. Television's status as an art form with neither art nor form leaves the medium vulnerable to attack on all sides. Everyone, it seems, wants a piece of the action.

Including the Reverend Jerry Falwell, who uses television as a personal platform on which to brighten his self-created image as moral knight in shining armor. On the other side of the arena stands Ed Asner, long an obscure character actor suddenly thrust into the limelight via two hit television series. Asner bestowed upon himself the mantle of leader, the liberal beacon willing to leap into the political, neorevolutionary war at home. Like so many other actors and actresses on television, Asner seems seduced by his own popularity, an amalgam of actor and act. While Ed Asner plays moral editor for the liberal faction in the country, he is repeating what so many of his fellow actors have done: using star status to elevate personal image. Raymond Burr, television's Perry Mason, and Veronica Hamel of "Hill Street Blues" are invited to speak before legal conventions. Jack Webb addresses law enforcement groups. Jack Klugman lectures on forensics. Almost as if in response to the accusations of TV as a vast wasteland, celebrities seek to justify their self-worth through what is essentially, a masterly blend of public service and public relations.

Somehow, in spite of all the threats, counter-threats, maneuvering and out-maneuvering, the season did manage to limp on to the tube. Most of the shows were predictable, some were surprisingly refreshing, one even managed to be outstanding—"Magnum, P.I.," by far the most imaginative television series since "The Fugitive." Here was Magnum (Tom Selleck) continually bathing himself, cleansing his body and perhaps his soul in the beautiful waters of the green Pacific, off the shores of the paradisaic beaches of Hawaii, an image perhaps more cleansing, more religious than anything the send-me-your-money Falwells could ever imagine. It was an image that evoked the dawn of leaving the serenity of water for the madness of civilization. It was an image that also evoked the specific dilemma of Magnum—detective drop-out—who could find peace and refreshment out of the "mainstream" only to return to the utter absurdity of paradise corrupt. The more ridiculous the weekly situations became, the more provocative the noirish series appeared, complete with forties movie-style narration delivered by Selleck with a gentleness that revealed the man beneath the muscles.

So we turn now to one season, a season with no physical beginning, middle, or end. We turn to the industrial continuum of American television, our most-watched but least-examined medium. This season has no climax of fall colors, no wintry snows, no humid summer nights. Instead, this is a climax of kinky kinetics, a phosphorous dance turning crazily from comedy to tragedy to action, twisting finally to static. It is a season of transitions.

In this twirl of the electronic ballet we take our turn and tune in.

1 Moral Majors—1

If the biggest question on everyone's lips in 1980 was who killed J.R., the biggest puzzle of 1981 was who brought forth J.F.—Jerry Falwell, head of the Moral Majority. This organization came thundering down the antenna in the summer of 1981, when, through a series of expertly coordinated broadcasts, telephone campaigns, mass appeals and mass mailings it managed to make a dent in the fall election. The "Silent Majority" of the seventies had, seemingly, found its voice. As the lights went out on the political careers of such long-term liberals as George McGovern, Birch Bayh, and Frank Church, one name seemed to spell victory for those who believed and damnation (Fall Well!) for those who didn't.

The November elections were a clear victory for the right, and the sloganable "Moral Majority" became a familiar topic for political pundits everywhere. "Thinkpieces" sprang up in respectable journals, television journalists contemplated the phenomenon over the air, and Jerry Falwell's ratings went up as television began its now familiar self-destructive action of creating the very monster intent on gobbling it up.*

Jerry Falwell was no stranger to television. He was the host of his own Sunday syndicated tune-to-God-and-contribute show, attracting, by his estimation (others would put the figures lower), fifteen to thirty million viewers a week over more than four hundred affiliated stations (more than half the affiliates in the country).

Now, in the flush of the Moral Majority's political success, the question became, where would Jerry Falwell strike his lightning next? The answer came soon enough. Falwell and company, including Pat Robertson and James Robison, along with Paul Weyrich and Richard Viguerie (Viguerie more political than evangelical), combined forces with a less well known minister, Robert E. Wildmon. Together, they set their sights on the television industry itself. It was even whispered that Falwell and company were considering the purchase of one of the networks. Falwell was quoted by Ben Stein in the February 1981 *Saturday Review,* as saying: "We have to change the kind of coverage that the network news gives to issues. We're sick of the humanistic bias on the news. There's too much in favor of abortion, too much about evolution and nothing about Creation. We want a nightly network news show which will let people know that they should place their reliance in God, and not in man as an animal."

According to *Newsweek,* by December 1980, Falwell was on his way, with the assistance of billionaires Bunker Hunt, Cullen Davis, and the Rockefellers, to perhaps take over one of the big three commercial networks. The idea wasn't that far out anymore once the dollar boys were willing to chip in. For $150 million it was possible to buy

---

*Joe McCarthy, Spiro Agnew, and Richard Nixon are just a few who attacked TV, using it to get their message across, gaining substantial power in the process.

enough stock to gain controlling interest in ABC, CBS, or NBC. Toward the end of the month a final, apocalyptic meeting between Jerry Falwell and Robert E. Wildmon took place in the back room of Falwell's home-based church in Lynchburg, Virginia. Wildmon gave his support for an all-out organized attack on the excessive sex, violence, and, as he termed it, pornographic attitude of network programming. Falwell's Moral Majority now became an arm of the Reverend Wildmon's burgeoning Coalition for Better Television, which quickly grew to include more than four hundred religious and civic organizations. The coalition was dedicated to conquering the networks through an economic boycott of products advertised on the shows they deemed unsuitable for their collective congregation's moral consumption.

A boycott was a proven tactic designed to hit the corporate body where it would hurt—in the pocketbook. It had been done once before to the networks, and for a time had worked. That was the fifties, when television was an infant, filled with old movies and wooden puppets. It was a nervous period of American history, described best by Stefan Kanfer in his penetrating study, *A Journal of the Plague Years.** This was the paranoid age of blacklisting, led by two self-appointed zealots. One was Vincent Hartnett, publisher of the notorious "Red Channels," the official approval sheet delineating who could work and who couldn't. Hartnett was characterized once by Michael Harrington as "the perfect spoiled-priest type."

The other was Theodore Kirkpatrick, with his publication "Counterattack." Together, Hartnett and Kirkpatrick conceived the notion of economic boycott against the networks. It was a powerful action. In the fifties, the advertising structure of the networks was even more cen-

---

*Stefan Kanfer, *A Journal of the Plague Years*, New York, Atheneum, 1973.

tral than it is today. Sponsors sought identification (and sales) through long-term associations with well-known personalities: Arthur Godfrey and Lipton Tea, Jack Benny and Lucky Strike, Ed Sullivan and Lincoln-Mercury.

General Foods, the big power of the day, owned numerous shows and was affiliated with countless stars. Therefore, General Foods became the logical first target, singled out for its enormous influence, and it was among the first to cave in to consumer pressure. It began shedding itself of any celebrity who might have the slightest taint. *Those dirty rings. They tried scrubbing them out, bleaching them out....*

The blacklisting era eventually faded when the networks found a way to battle the power of the corporate-advertising branch of broadcasting. Single-unit sponsorship was eventually phased out and replaced by "spot" purchases of ad space. This is why a program like "The Tonight Show" might have as many as fifty different sponsors in a week's worth of shows, with another fifty at the local, or affiliate, level. Carson is identified with no single product, or group of products. If one sponsor wants to drop off the bandwagon for any reason, there are dozens ready to buy into the massive "Tonight Show" audience's view.

Still, while the economic boycott was in effect during the fifties, the careers of many stars—including William Loeb, Canada Lee, and Mady Christians—were rinsed down the drain. It may have only worked for a while, but it worked. The operative factor in those days was "loyalty," and the same is true today. If, in the fifties, loyalty meant allegiance to a particular form of government, in the 1981–1982 season it clearly meant allegiance to a particular form of higher being.

This thirty-year trip from government to God wasn't all that unlikely, or unguided. In the sixties and seventies, Billy Graham could be seen at the White House, giving his blessings to Richard Nixon. Nixon himself first came into power delving into "Communist activities" while still in Congress. His political future would benefit from coming out on the side of the angels.

If television made such an easy target in the fifties, at least part of the blame has to be put on the industry itself, for the way it shivered in the wind and caught cold so easily. CBS, the primary target of so much of the blacklist, exemplified the panic and capitulation of the networks. On the one hand there was Edward R. Murrow standing up to McCarthyism. On the other hand, there was CBS, knuckling under to the commandments of "Red Channels" and "Counterattack."

Falwell and Wildmon wasted no time. By January 1981, half a million questionaires were mailed to chapter affiliates and suborganizations of the new coalition. Some of the questions asked about individual programs were:

1. Was this a program that would be enjoyed by the entire family?

2. Would the program help build good character in youth and children?

3. Would viewing the program help promote a better family life?

Lists of approved and disapproved shows were drawn up and distributed, with the names of sponsors alongside. Finally, in the early spring, a consumer boycott was formally announced. Fifteen million consumers were earmarked by the coalition to receive, via a well-organized mail campaign, material that would advise them which products to buy—and which to avoid.

Among the first shows affected by the mere announcement of the boycott were "Three's Company" and "Too Close for Comfort," both coming under the coalition's category of "jiggle," both on ABC, both big in the

Nielsens, both very targetable. Since a thirty-second spot on these two shows cost approximately $137,000, a determined defection could prove costly. While many advertisers were coming out publicly against any so-called boycott, there was a sudden, increased sponsor rush to buy time on such "jiggle-free" shows as the reliable "Sixty Minutes," whose commercial fees jumped to better than $175,000 per thirty seconds. Ralston-Purina went on record, publicizing its time-buying intentions: "Little House on the Prairie," "M*A*S*H," "Magnum, P.I.," "Love Boat," and "Fantasy Island." In fact, "Three's Company" and "Too Close for Comfort" were having trouble, despite their popularity, selling out their commercial spots.

The first approach the networks used to counter-attack the boycott was outrage and outcry. James Duffy, president of ABC Television, told *Newsweek:* "They would like to control the content of television. They seek to use their view of morality not just as a code of conduct in their own lives, but to impose it on everyone else." Fred Silverman, the soon-to-be-deposed president of NBC, called the coalition "a sneak-attack on the foundation of democracy."

Dubious democracy notwithstanding, TV Row (that high-rise strip along Sixth Avenue in New York long noted for its interference with broadcast signals from the Empire State Building and the World Trade Center) promptly announced a series of cancellations on the fall schedule. Slated to go were "Soap" and "Charlie's Angels," two long-time, sexy anchors of the ABC schedule. "Love, Sidney," a new sit-com in which Tony Randall played a homosexual, was, according to NBC, "undergoing changes," meaning that all references to Sidney's being gay were being deleted from future episodes, if the show got on the schedule at all. "Vega$," the ABC action-adventure show, was canceled. So were "Lobo" and "Enos"—two more below-the-neck comedies.

The problem with fighting the boycott was that in

some ways it had put its finger on . . . something. Sex, as
perceived by the networks, was indeed disfigured; titillation had replaced intimacy. Even jeans commercials were
hotter than hell. The boycott also happened to be per-
fectly legal. Back in the fifties, the beginning of the end
for "Red Channels" and "Counterattack" and their domination of the television networks was the celebrated libel
case brought by John Henry Falk against Vincent Hartnett. Defended by Louis Nizer, Falk proved that he'd
been wrongly singled out by "Red Channels" as a Communist. The question of the networks' complicity in the
use of a blacklist remained a freaky sideshow in this three-
ring circus of a trial.

If things had gotten out of hand in the fifties, it was
because no one had any real idea just how far things could
go. Both sides were blissful amateurs. By the eighties,
though, the warriors had turned pro. The Reverend Falwell had discovered a way to raise millions on television
through the effective use of the medium's exposure. It was
a logical step from money to power, one the coalition
seemed intent on taking. So secure were the leaders of the
boycott that they publicly called for the American Civil
Liberties Union to endorse their actions. They wanted the
ACLU to agree with the coalition that people have the
right to spend their money as they wish. Censorship? Not
at all, said the coalition. Let the networks show what they
want. Let the sponsors sponsor what they want. And let
the buyers buy what they want.

Reagonomics in action.

By June, The Coalition for Better Television claimed
that five million Americans were committed to partici-
pate in a boycott, with twenty million more a phone call
away. On the heels of the coalition's pronouncements,
Procter and Gamble said that it would refuse to sponsor
shows it regarded as excessively violent, filled with profanity, or "too sexual." The company made no secret of its

new guidelines. They were disclosed publicly by Owen B. Butler, the chairman of Procter and Gamble's board, addressing the Academy of Television Arts and Sciences in Hollywood. In addition, Butler told the Academy, "We think the coalition is expressing some very important and broadly held views about gratuitous sex, violence and profanity. I can assure you we are listening very carefully to what they say, and I urge you to do the same. The problem which they and we believe exists must be solved by mutual understanding, and not by confrontation." All in all, Procter and Gamble pulled its commercials off fifty network television programs.

"Pleased," was the way Reverend Wildmon put it when asked for his reaction to Butler's comments. In fact, Wildmon revealed, he'd been given a copy of the speech in advance. What wasn't revealed, though, was the wheeling and dealing the networks were now attempting with the advertisers. Rumors of "premiums" for ad space on "clean shows" were everywhere. The network response? Television works on supply and demand. . . .

The same week that Owen Butler addressed the Academy, The National Coalition on Television Violence announced that "violence was up 16 percent" in prime time during 1980–1981 as compared with the previous year. "Riker," a show about the adventures of a modern-day police officer, on CBS, was deemed by the coalition to be the most violent network prime-time show of the season. It was not renewed. The coalition announced that the show displayed "an average" of thirty-five violent acts per hour. NBC's "Walking Tall" came in second with "an average" of twenty-five violent acts per episode. "Walking Tall" was not renewed. The ten most violent shows (according to the coalition) still on the fall schedule were listed by them as follows:

1. "Foul Play"*		ABC
2. "Vega$"		ABC
3. "Lobo"*		NBC

 4. "The Greatest American Hero" ABC
 5. "The Incredible Hulk"*   CBS
 6. "Concrete Cowboys"*   CBS
 7. "Magnum, P.I."   CBS
 8. "Hart to Hart"   ABC
 9. "The Dukes of Hazzard"   CBS
10. "BJ and the Bear"*   NBC

Five of these shows (marked with an asterisk) were abruptly canceled by the start of the new season. "Vega$" was canceled early in the season; "The Dukes of Hazzard" was in trouble by the end of the season, with cancellation expected.† "Hart to Hart" was on the brink of extinction until the untimely deaths of William Holden and Natalie Wood, the lover and wife, respectively, of the costars of the show, proved to be a curiosity factor worthy of a boost in ratings and renewed life in prime time. That left only "The Greatest American Hero" and "Magnum, P.I." apparently unscathed by the coalition.

Meanwhile, the twelve and one-half billion dollars advertisers were to spend this season on network shows were being put, for the most part, where there was the least chance of clashing with the coalition. The ad rates for thirty-second spots for "Sixty Minutes" and "Dallas" were the most expensive, at $175,000. The top five shows per ad rate came in as "Sixty Minutes," "Dallas," and "M*A*S*H" (CBS)—$137,500; "Three's Company"*

---

†The cast was entirely replaced for the 1982–83 season.

*The appearance of "Three's Company" seems at first glance to weaken the argument. However, it should be remembered that the show, for a while, had considerable trouble selling out its spots. When the star of the series, Suzanne Sommers, walked off the show in a contract dispute, her miscalculation of the situation was a break for the producers. Ms. Sommers was the focal point of the show's "jiggling." She was promptly fired, replaced by Priscilla Barnes, a far less flashy actress, while the scripts shifted their focus onto the decidedly non-jiggling John Ritter. At this point, the series began to fill its fall roster with commercial spots.

(ABC)—$110,000; and "20/20" (ABC)—$100,000. It's interesting that "20/20" rarely broke into the top fifteen shows, yet its revenue rate was higher than "Mork and Mindy," a show that drew higher ratings. Finally, "NBC Magazine," the lowest-rated show for the better part of the 1980–1981 season, came in at $70,000 per thirty-second spot, higher than 60 percent of the shows in prime time.

If no one at the networks was willing to take a strong stand against the Reverends Falwell and Wildmon, there was life among the independent producers of Hollywood. Appropriately enough, the first producer to make a statement against the coalition and the proposed boycott was Lee Rich, of Lorimar Productions. Lorimar was the developer and production company responsible for "Dallas," a target of the coalition protected, for the moment, only by its position as the number-one program in America. Lee Rich, shortly after the "violence report" was made public by the Reverend Wildmon, said, "I don't need the Moral Majority or Reverend Wildmon to tell me what to watch. . . . Wildmon is like Hitler with his hit list. Who is to say that Wildmon . . . is the judge. When does it stop?"

The networks, though, were playing it cool. In late June, ABC Vice-President Alfred Schneider claimed that the reason for the curtailment of "jiggling" on ABC sitcoms was that the viewers were pulling back from that sort of programming. Joel Segal, of the Ted Bates Agency, one of the major television advertisement placers, stated that while Procter and Gamble was pulling out of some TV shows, it had nothing to do with the coalition. "General Hospital," he pointed out, had gotten a cover of *Time* magazine, and not a word had come from any coalitions. The Reverend Wildmon assured his followers that daytime TV "is not where the action is." The question was, the action for whom? Attack a prime-time show, you get prime-time attention. Attack a day-time soap, you get homemakers and college students.

Soon after the "violence list" came another statement, this one from Terence Cardinal Cooke, calling for New York Catholics to pressure the networks against the continuation of "destructive television programming." The Cardinal went on to implore Catholics to contribute to a "Catholic Communications Fund" to combat "the weekly diet of violence, distorted sexuality and the glorification of attitudes which are selfish and opposed to the common good. When necessary, as has always been the case, I recommend that you express your objections to destructive television programming."

As Lee Rich continued to oppose the coalition and its tactics, the networks released a remarkable study, conducted by ABC, entitled "Programming and the Viewer: The Right to Choose." The study showed that the members of the Moral Majority watched the same shows that nonmembers watched. If this was supposed to deflate Wildmon and Falwell, it wasn't a very smart tactic. Of course they watched the same shows, the coalition leaders said. That was the whole point: anyone turning on the television couldn't help but see all the sex and violence on the air. ABC's report hung like a bad odor waiting to be eliminated by a moral blast of air freshener.

Another independent voice opposing Falwell and Wildmon was Norman Lear's. Lear had been singled out as early as February 1981 by Jerry Falwell as the "single most villainous member of the decadent powers" that controlled the networks. Lear, television's resident liberal, wanted to fight ire with fire. He announced a campaign of his own, designed to advertise to the country the "anti-democratic actions of moral majoritarians." He planned a series of short, commercial spots featuring such stars as Carol Burnett, Goldie Hawn, and Muhammad Ali reminding TV viewers of Americans' right to free speech and free thought. As soon as Lear announced his intention to make his commercials, Falwell announced that he and the coalition would match Lear "spot for spot." It was open warfare now, with Madison Avenue supplying the weaponry for the brand-name battle for democracy. Selling products with commercials was, after all, what Madison Avenue did best.

Battlecries from the front continued to pour out of the mouths of the generals. Jerry Falwell: "You can't be a good Christian and a liberal at the same time."

Bill Moyers: "Our democracy cannot agree to a 'Moral Majority' that makes sectarian doctrine the test of political opinion. You may have that only where all are alike in thought and root and intent, which America is not."

Richard Viguerie: "We've already taken control of the conservative movement. And conservatives have taken control of the Republican Party. The remaining thing is to see if we can control the country."

Norman Lear: "The danger of the Religious New Right is not that they are speaking out on political issues, which is their right, if not their obligation; it is the way they attack the integrity and character of anyone who does not stand with them."

As the hour of the boycott approached, TV advertisers were scattering like roaches from Raid to avoid being named on a rumored July "hit-list," supposed to already include Smith Kline & French Laboratories, Warner-Lambert Company, Beecham, Inc., Esmark, Inc., Miles Laboratories, Inc., and Sterling Drugs, Inc. Coalition "committees" and splinter groups were forming daily. The National Federation for Decency, newly formed and newly informative, specifically cited Warner-Lambert, Beecham, American Motors Corp., Gulf & Western, Noxell Corp., and Pfizer, Inc. as sponsors of shows that were "sexually offensive." "Three's Company," "Soap," "Laverne and Shirley," "Happy Days," "Taxi," and "Too Close for Comfort" were deemed by the group to be programs "not suitable for prime time because of their sexual nature." Shows cited for their "excessive profanity, including the use of such terms as 'damn,' 'God,' 'Jesus,' and 'bastard,' " were "Soap," "M*A*S*H," "Archie Bunker's Place," "It's a Living," "Too Close for Comfort," "Flo," "The Jeffersons," "The White Shadow," and several made-for-TV movies.

There was more. The coalition announced, a few days later in July, that the following sponsors were guilty of advertising on "the most violent shows": Mazda, 7-11 Stores, Johnson & Johnson, Frito-Lay, Inc., L'Eggs Products, and Phillips Petroleum Company. Sources from TV Row told of "purge" meetings being conducted in Madison Avenue conference rooms to try to reconcile differences between the coalition and the advertisers. Finally, Jack Sholl, a representative of the Warner-Lambert Company, confirmed the existence of these purges in the pages of *The New York Times:* "One reason for accepting the invitation to the meeting was to see what they wanted. It's been our long-standing posture to be willing to sit down and talk with responsible groups and parties interested in the activities of the corporation."

Just when it seemed that the eighties were indeed going to explode into the fifties, the coalition suddenly announced that it was leaning toward postponement of the upcoming boycott. On June 30, the coalition officially set the plan aside indefinitely. The Reverend Wildmon declared at a press conference that the boycott was "no longer necessary," that meetings with executives of the advertising corporations had demonstrated that they were in basic agreement with the coalition. This was a truly astonishing turn of events. The coalition was declaring a victory before the war had officially begun! Wildmon and his group had succeeded in scaring the corporations into submission. The ants, with a few well-placed pushes, were able to roll over the elephant. It seemed at this juncture that the coalition was going to get everything it wanted, and perhaps more, using merely the threat of retribution.

Still, the coalition wasn't satisfied. Reverend Falwell announced that his organization, the Moral Majority, was in the process of "raising funds for a war chest to buy and assist others in buying full-page ads across the nation naming public enemy #1, or #2, or #3—or whoever they are, and listing their products." Singled out for praise by Falwell was Procter and Gamble, the advertiser who had been the first to pull out of more than fifty scheduled fall shows. Still no mention was made of Procter and Gamble's extensive ownership and sponsorship of the daytime soaps, where sex and violence continued to flourish.

Was Jerry Falwell a man filled with confidence, flush with the power of success? Falwell: "Give me Adolf Hitler for ten minutes and I'll have him saying Amen."

Indeed there seemed to be no end to the pressure tactics of Falwell and the coalition during the coming season. Yet while the moral right was coming down hard on the content of television, the angry left was coming down even harder on the business of broadcasting.

2 Strike!

After several decades of relative peace, the Hollywood entertainment unions erupted in 1980 as the first of a series of strikes hit tinseltown. For thirteen weeks in 1980, the Screen Actors Guild (SAG) struck the TV and movie studios, embattled in a series of conflicts culminating in a single, dominating issue: future royalty scales for ancillary venues not in existence when the now-expiring contracts were originally ratified. Cable TV and cassettes were the heart of the matter. Simply put, the actors wanted to be paid every time a film (or TV show) appeared on cable or pay-TV, and to receive royalties on the sale or rental of cassettes.

The last time this problem had come to a head was thirty years earlier, when the TV networks found a cheap and abundant source of programming in the vaults of movie studios. Thirty-five years of Hollywood's finest were rented out and played again and again on television. Since no provisions for television airing had been included in anyone's contract when the films were made (commercial television didn't exist before 1946), no actors, directors, or writers were paid royalties. Many of the biggest TV stars of the fifties spent their last years in virtual poverty. Such luminaries as Stan Laurel and Bud Abbott wound up penniless while their old films entertained a whole new generation of fans.

Eventually, a provision was included in all new contracts for payments to actors who appeared in films made after 1948—a compromise questionable in its fairness, accepted by the unions to keep peace and presumably to keep their members working. This problem was resolved at the height of the fifties blacklisting, when the unions were being torn apart by federal investigation and advertising pressure on the networks. No one wanted a prolonged battle over contracts at the time; they were more concerned with keeping television a viable form of private enterprise.

One of the results of the fifties' turmoil in the entertainment industry was the general depoliticizing of the entertainment unions. Up until the infamous jailing of "the Hollywood 10," the Hollywood unions had been decidedly political. As early as 1931, when the Writers Guild was formed—in spite of extreme pressure from MGM and Irving Thalberg—the unions were marked as political hotbeds. Thalberg threatened any writer who defected from what were, in effect, writing sweatshops, with lifelong disbarment from all studios. From the thirties through the fifties, the political fervor that swept the entertainment unions was unparalled in any other industry. However, after HUAC, Representative Nixon, the arrest and imprisonment of the Hollywood 10, and the enforcement of the blacklist, the unions were reduced to little more than dues-collecting, apolitical, closed shops.*

---

*For the best, most complete history of unionism in Hollywood, see Larry Ceplair and Steven Englund, *The Inquisition in Hollywood*, New York, Anchor Press/Doubleday, 1980.

This all changed in 1980, though, when SAG, unable to satisfactorily resolve what it saw as a replay of the fifties royalties problem, did what the studios assumed to be the unthinkable, let alone the undoable. SAG pulled a general strike, bringing virtually all film and television production to a halt.

Every movement seems to produce a leader, and the new union movement was no exception. Ed Asner of "Lou Grant" fame emerged as the dominant force among the striking actors. For many years the heavy in Hollywood feature films, one of those faces without names, Asner seemed forever destined to be a character actor. Overweight, short, balding, and decidedly not "pretty," he was one of hundreds who made a career out of working here and there, with stardom seemingly forever out of reach. However, things turned around for him in 1970, when Grant Tinker and Mary Tyler Moore cast him as the brutish-but-lovable local news producer Lou Grant in "The Mary Tyler Moore Show," thrusting Asner into unexpected stardom. So popular was the Lou Grant character that, in 1978, when Mary Tyler Moore decided to close the shop on her series, MTM Enterprises (her company) decided to create a new series using him. Lou Grant left Minneapolis for Los Angeles, swapping local TV for a job as the editor of a fictitious Los Angeles newspaper not unlike the *Los Angeles Times.* Lou Grant also left behind his sense of humor. Suddenly, we were presented with the "new" Lou: self-righteous, wise, becalming, intelligent. Oddly, as Asner's appearances at strike meetings and rallies increased, it began to get harder and harder to tell exactly who was doing all the talking and shouting—Ed Asner or new Lou. Lou Grant was in danger of becoming the Jerry Falwell of labor.

The similarities between the two far outweighed the differences. Both claimed to represent massive numbers of silent but loyal followers. Both claimed moral responsibility as their ultimate motivation. Both had series on television where they played wise if preachy characters. And now both were on the news every night. It looked for all the world like a political campaign.

Asner made his position plain. He wanted fair guarantees for the poor, underpaid actors to insure that they weren't ripped off by cable companies and cassette distributors. The issue, according to Asner, was simple—cut and dried.

Only it wasn't. The history of unionism in the entertainment industry reveals that often it is the performers who benefit least from political activism. Actor's Equity, the union that represents Broadway talent, is a good example. Theater historians (and out-of-work actors) will tell you that Equity contracts have become so restrictive, so prohibitive, that the primary reason fewer and fewer shows are being done, both on Broadway and off, is that producers simply can't meet the requirements laid down by the unions. A single, one-set musical must now be budgeted in the three-million-dollar range to be produced on Broadway. Big dollars mean small risks. Stars are obligatory, casts have to be kept small, sets designed to minimize the need for union stagehands. The musician's union has been known to let a show close because a producer won't agree to employ a minimum number of musicians, even if they are to be paid as "walkers," meaning collectors of paychecks for no other reason than that the union insists they be hired. Many "walkers" never even bother to show up for nightly performances, stopping by weekly to pick up their checks.

All of this translates to a brutal reality: that along with union security for the established comes less opportunity for the unknown. Taken to Hollywood, the situation becomes even more tenuous. If union regulations force greater payouts to actors, producers will increasingly go with "bankable" stars on the order of, say, an Ed Asner. A star might then mean the difference between a "go" and a "no." In reality, Ed Asner was picketing for Ed Asner, even as the cherubic acting-school graduates hoisting him on their shoulders as their savior were smiling brightly for the news cameras. The eventual settlement of the SAG strike made one thing clear. Most producers would be less inclined to go with an unknown. Giving a new kid a break had become too expensive a risk. Yet, a year later, during the height of Falwellmania, there was Ed Asner, rallying yet another union, the Writers Guild (WGA). Only this time there was a difference. Asner was now preparing to run for president of the Screen Actors Guild, the same position once held by another actor—Ronald Reagan.

The writers walked away from their typewriters on April 11, 1981, just as most scripts were due for delivery in preparation for the 1981–1982 television season. I should state here that I am a member of the Writers Guild West, having written for prime-time television. In fact, I was caught in the conflict of spring 1981, during which time I resigned from a writing job in Hollywood, refusing to cross a picket line. While I supported the intentions of the Guild then, and do now, I believe the internal dissension between unions was a major factor in the failure of the WGA to attain the terms for which it picketed.

The leaders of the writers strike believed that the walkout would be a short one, that the studios had "learned their lesson" from the SAG strike and would be more amenable to cutting a workable deal. Yet, as the weeks dragged on, there was absolutely no movement from either side. The writers were holding out for the expiration of the Directors Guild (DGA) contract, due to run out July 1. It had been unofficially agreed on by the two guilds that if the WGA hadn't settled on a workable contract by then, the DGA would join the picket line.

The writers in Hollywood are a different bunch than the actors. The WGA was the first organized, and most political, of all Hollywood unions. Ten writers went to prison in the fifties for refusing to answer questions by HUAC, not ten actors. It was, and is, the writers who have traditionally stood at the bottom of Hollywood's hierarchy, and for a very practical reason. Writers don't have fans. Writers don't control shows. Writers don't even control their own scripts. Most often, a writer who does a pilot script will never do another episode of the series if the show goes into weekly production. If the actors' strike was a "cute" news item, with middle America scratching its head trying to understand how all those stars had the nerve to strike when they were making thousands of dollars a week, the writer's strike was a rude behind-the-scenes battle, causing as much dissent as solidarity in the industry. Mac St. John, representative of the International Alliance of Theatrical State Employees (a craft guild operating within the studios) commented angrily that "some of my people haven't worked since the actor's strike." A full 50 percent of IATSE's members had remained out of work since the 1980 SAG strike. In 1981, with production shut down once again, those who depended on the entertainment industry for their survival were hurting badly. Restaurants complained of a lack of business; talent unions were in danger of going under. Off the record, everyone seemed to know why the studios were in no hurry to settle things with the writers, why the studios weren't the least bit threatened if the directors decided that they, too, wanted to take a hike.

During the actors' strike, it became apparent that the studios could simply replay episodes of their most popular shows, lease previously unsold pilots to the networks, or re-lease recent movies to television and to the theaters, collecting hugh revenues without having to pay out huge producton costs. In fact, the studios were saving vast amounts of money by laying off craft workers and virtu-

ally all its nonunion personnel—secretaries and mainte-
nance operators—while continuing to collect income.
There was a big dollar difference between paying out a
residual and financing a production.

While the Directors Guild publicly supported the
spirit of the Writers Guild walkout, privately it was being
pressured by IATSE and other guilds to settle things before July 1. Days before the DGA was scheduled to go out
on strike, it announced that a settlement had been
reached with the studios and producers, thereby preserv-
ing its forty-eight-year history of strikeless existence. Two
weeks later, the WGA caved in, its members ratifying by
an overwhelming vote ("unanimous" according to guild
spokesman Shannon Boyd) a contract far short of the
guild's original demands.

The pact gave writers 2 percent of the gross of shows
made expressly for pay-TV *after the producer recouped
his investment.* A figure of $1 million an hour for video-
taped presentations and $1.25 million for live shows was
set as the break-even point for the producers. A writer's
base pay was increased by 65.8 percent over the four-year
life of the new contract. Minimum pay for a one-hour
television show rose from $9,434, to $14,318. Fees for
writing a major theatrical movie went from $26,326 to an
eventual $40,000.

The terms were essentially identical with those
agreed on by the DGA, except that the DGA had been
able to eliminate the producers' break-even point. Pay-
ment for directors was scheduled to begin at the 100,000
unit sales mark for disk and cassettes, *regardless of
whether the producer had made his money back.* In other
words, the directors had eliminated the mandatory producer's break-even point that the writers had agreed to.
Without question, the Writers Guild felt bitter toward
what it considered a sellout by the Directors Guild. The
writers quickly pointed out that the WGA contract encouraged further cost-cutting (translation: lack of employ-

ment). A producer able to bring in a show for $200,000 saw a potential $800,000 profit before the writers saw a penny. And who could trust a producer? The cost of audits and distribution follow-ups would cut into any eventual profits the writers might see.

The DGA, in turn, was even quicker to point out that during the strike, residuals paid to WGA members (monies paid to writers for reruns, repeats, and sales of pilots) were up 38.1 percent in May 1981, 21.3 percent in June. Look, they said, we did you writers a big favor. We settled things just as your residuals were beginning to run out!

A curious footnote to the strike-torn preseason was the day that Ed Asner crossed the musicians' union picket line to report for work on "Lou Grant." Almost unnoticed among the other strikes was the musicians' walkout—unnoticed and still unsettled even as the writers and directors were gearing up for the fall season. There was Ed Asner, voice of the little people, and there was the picket line—the little people themselves. At first, Asner put CBS and MTM Enterprises on notice that he wouldn't cross the line until the musicians were dealt with. CBS countered with a threat to cancel the "Lou Grant" series. To the mute disbelief of everyone who had stood beside Asner (and to many who had stood against him), Asner quietly reported for duty. Questioned on his actions, Asner would reply that, yes, he did cross the picket line, and, yes, he was ashamed of himself.

3 Cable

Although it is generally assumed that cable TV is a recent
phenomenon, the fact is that cable was around and in use
even before color television. In many regions of the country, cable was the only way a signal could be received
because of high mountain interference or powerful elec-
tromagnetic displacement from energy plant operations.
The cable "revolution" of the late seventies and early
eighties came after the development of the micronic
cable, an ultrathin wire with the ability to carry hundreds
of stations, paving the way for potentially unlimited
sources of revenue. Once cable became economically feasible, the "Gold Rush of '81" was on.

Almost as soon as the cable boom hit, the networks
began to organize against having their programming
wired through the various systems without due compen-
sation. The cable companies argued that they should be
paid for delivering network advertising to an ever-
increasing audience, which would in turn increase the per
capita ratings scale the networks used to set their commercial fees. It wasn't that bad an argument. Anyway, the

networks figured, pay-TV would never, could never, replace free broadcasting. Never.

1981 was the year *never* turned into *now.*

By the fall of 1981, more than fifty cable channels were available in most major broadcast markets. Territories in New York, Los Angeles, and Chicago were carved up by various cable operations, with the broad spectrum of programming a combination of free-with-cable channels and optional pay-cable networks. The sudden influx of new cable stations was caused mainly by the FCC's tacit approval of cable's right to broadcast network fare by endorsing a broader, nonregulated set of guidelines for "narrowcasting" (targeting a program to a specific audience). Satellites made it possible for one base of operations to sell its product around the globe, something that while technically feasible for the networks was still illegal by FCC standards. The entire structure of affiliated but independent stations was a highly regulated operation, created, in part, to prevent any one network from dominating the airwaves. However, the FCC attitude toward cable was quite different, decidedly more relaxed. It was as if the government were encouraging further competition, perceiving a further fractionalizing of the market.

The most attractive aspect of cable as a profit venture was specialization. Whereas the networks depended on the ratings to determine the size of their viewing audience, and therefore the scale of ad rates, cable stations could base their income on a prepaid umbrella structure. One system aligned with several cable distribution markets, collecting a fee from each, could operate at a profit with a relatively small audience. A network broadcast reaching two million viewers is a financial disaster. A cablecast reaching two million viewers can be highly profitable, depending on budgets and subscription fees.

Once the networks realized that cable wasn't going to go away, the corporate heads of the big three—ABC, CBS, and NBC—began lobbying Congress for more restrictive guidelines. They pressed, unsuccessfully, for the FCC to come down a little harder on the competition.

When that didn't work, the networks did the ony logical thing left to do. Instead of trying to fight the competition, they started buying it. During the 1981–1982 season, amid the disarray caused by the Moral Majority, The Coalition for Better Programming, and the industry strikes, the following cable networks were formed:

1. *ABC-Westinghouse.*   These two corporate giants announced the formation of two cable operations. The first was a feature-oriented, twenty-four-hour all-news network. The second had a more concise, headline format, delivering the news continuously in twenty-minute blocks of information.

2. *The ARTS Network.*   A joint effort of ABC's video division and the Hearst Corporation that was designed to carry commercial advertising so as to be offered free to cable users, the concept of ARTS was basically to import overseas television. The goal was to take over the "Mobil Showcase," which had been the basis for public television and was now floundering financially. "Mobil Showcase," had, in fact, been the pride of the energy megacorporation. However, Mobil sensed that part of the Public Broadcasting System's problems were due to the ever-expanding world of cable. Mobil's initial investment into the ARTS network was between $750,000 and $1 million.

3. *CBS Cable.*   "We'd like to expand your universe" was the way CBS announced its entry into the cable arena. Perhaps the most ambitious of the networks, CBS quickly incorporated 250 outlets for its operation. The programming is a continuum of dance, drama, music, interviews, and information. The station is on the air seven days a week, with nine of its daily twelve hours repeated in three-hour segments. Forty percent of the programming is slated to be European import. Advertising space

is available. Five minutes on CBS Cable can be purchased for $60,000. The Start-up cost for CBS was ten million dollars.*

4. *CBS-American Telephone and Telegraph.* Another CBS venture, which emphasizes home information. The eventual goal is electronic banking and shopping, with local and national display advertising. Generically, this type of cable is known as videotext.

The networks weren't the only ones snapping up the cables. Here are some of the other operations that came together in the 1981–1982 season:

5. *Walt Disney Productions and Westinghouse Broadcasting.* Another venture for Westinghouse, this operation was perceived as a sixteen-hours-per-day cable channel specializing in family entertainment. The initial start-up cost was $10 million.

6. *Dow Jones and Co.* The venerable Wall Street conglomerate acquired a 25 percent share of a Boston-based cable station, Continental Cablevision, the thirteenth largest cable system in the United States, servicing a half million subscribers in ten states. Dow Jones and Co. had previously tried, unsuccessfully, to acquire UA-Columbia Pictures Cablevision, along with the huge library of classic films the two Hollywood studios had. The agreement with Continental included the opportunity for Dow Jones to buy an additional one million shares at some future date, for the original *purchase-in* price of twenty-five dollars a share. Continental then with-

---

*In the fall of 1982, William Paley announced his retirement from CBS. Shortly thereafter, the network announced CBS Cable would be discontinued due to a lack of advertising revenue. CBS Cable became the first major cable failure.

drew two million shares it was about to put on the market.

7. *The United States Chamber of Commerce.* This system will beam live telecasts to business subscribers, via satellite, to be known as The American Business Network, or BIZNET. It will offer reports on business-related political, legislative, and regulatory developments. *One stated goal of BIZNET is to help probusiness candidates run for Congress.*

8. *The Entertainment Channel.* Affiliated with RKO-Nederlander Productions for the purpose of broadcasting current Broadway shows, the scheduled broadcast week consists of fifty-three hours: seven hours weekdays, nine weekends. It is underwritten by Rockefeller Center Cable, a subsidiary of Rockefeller Center and RCA Cable, a division of RCA Inc., which owns NBC-TV. The start-up investment was $5 million.

9. *The Turner Broadcasting System.* In addition to Ted Turner's Cable News Network, already cablecasting one year, Turner announced the formation of CNN 2, an ancillary news channel to deliver a compact, twenty-minute, revolving hard newscast. CNN 1 has an established viewing audience of eight million. Turner announced in late 1981 that he was looking for partners to expand his operation. It was estimated that the combined Ted Turner cable ventures were losing a million dollars a month. Turner claimed to be working toward operating in the black.

10. *The Playboy Channel.* Playboy Enterprises, a subsidiary of the Hugh Hefner publishing empire, in partnership with Escapade, an existing soft-core sex-oriented cable channel, announced a video version of Playboy Magazine. "Escapade" changed its name to The Playboy Channel.

11. *Bravo.*   This system presents mostly live musical presentations and middle- and high-brow classical performances. It has no commercials, and costs ten dollars per household per month.

12. *The Satellite Program Network.*   This network plans to incorporate four existing satellite networks for the combined presentation of international programming, feature films, business and religious programming, and general information.

13. *Warner-Amex Cable Communications.*   Already in existence for several seasons on a regional broadcast basis, WAMEX is the first cable operation with two-way capabilities, enabling polling and electronic game playing. One branch of Warner-Amex is Nickleodeon. This is programming aimed entirely at children, commercial-free, with an estimated daily audience of three million.

14. *Home Box Office.*   The pioneer in the presentation of uncut, unedited recent feature films, this service expanded after its first year of operation (1974) to include variety, on-location "event" programming. HBO is generally acknowledged as the first successful pay-TV venture. The plusses are repeated commercial-free screenings of the films. The negatives are some of the films—often so bad they've never seen the light of a projector in a theater. HBO is a subsidiary of Time-Life, Inc.

15. *The Z Station.*   Los Angeles's boutique answer to the giant HBO. Simply sensational, Z has consistently presented the best movies combined with the smartest scheduling. A big bonus is the once-a-year airing of films nominated for Academy Awards.

16. *Cinemax.*   Another subsidiary of Time-Life, Cinemax is essentially a repetition of HBO, with the addition of a few more movies and the elimination of variety

shows. While there is an ongoing competition for the twenty-six cable channels currently available in the New York area, Time-Life is able to offer two pay-TV channels, while cable ventures that are available in other markets on an access basis (no additional fees) can't get a slot.

17. *Showtime.* Another movies-for-pay outlet, of which Viacom, the free-TV syndicator of those series no longer on the networks, owns 50 percent. The good money says Showtime will eventually be an outlet for a TV "repertory" consisting mainly of Viacom-owned shows.

18. *The Cable Health Network.* Also owned by Viacom, this outlet specializes in health and medical reports, twenty-four hours a day. If you're wondering whatever happened to Regis Philbin, look no further.

19. *The Weather Channel.* It operates twenty-four hours a day, seven days a week.

20. *The Eternal World Network.* On the air twenty-four hours a day, seven days a week (including Sunday), the channel is run by thirteen nuns. "Most people think we're a little touched in the head," Mother Angelica announced to the press, adding that she was sure the station would succeed "with a lot of help from the Lord."

21. *Video Newscasting Network.* A biweekly tape running approximately forty minutes offers across-the-board information on business, entertainment, and soft news, magazine-style. It is available by station subscription, on an access basis.

Even though each of the three networks had bought in, there was still a fair amount of apprehension along TV Row about the enormous growth of the cable industry. Defections were occurring daily. Producers were leaving the networks in droves, anxious to get in on the ground floor of what was obviously the coming trend. Norman Lear announced his intention to expand T.A.T., his production company, to include extensive cable programming. He openly urged the government and the FCC to deal lightly with cable regulations. He spoke with authority and with the vocal support of women, blacks, Asians, hispanics, even paraplegics; a powerful constituency made up of those least satisfied with what they considered should be their fair share of the establishment pie.

While Lear pressed the progressive buttons, the networks stepped up their pressure. They feared a severe loss of profits if they couldn't guarantee their affiliate stations exclusive quality programming. After all, the network executives figured, how soon would it be before affiliates dropped the networks and joined the cable stations, turning a seller's market into a buyer's market? Traditionally, affiliates had only three networks from which to buy new programming; now there was a potentially unlimited amount of programming to be had. As the country continued to wire itself to receive, the networks were looking for a way to pull the plug on the competition.

Finally, as the season began, there evolved what became known along TV Row as the "Great Cable Compromise." It involved the networks, the affiliates, The Motion Picture Association of America, and the National Association of Broadcasters. A "protection list" of up to three hundred movies per station was drawn, for which exclusive rights were to be held by the networks. These films were off-limits to cable, and the list was to be updated every three months. TV series, including those sold to syndication, were protected from cable for the life of the station's contract right to broadcast. Any cable system serving three thousand or fewer subscribers was exempt. This last provision was included to preserve the original function of cable, to deliver programming to areas not able to receive normal TV signals.

These guidelines, set down by the FCC, brought with them new problems, such as the rush to buy "dishes," a direct result of the "under three thousand" clause. Dishes are actually satellite signal-receivers, very expensive and very cumbersome. Yet they began popping up in back yards all over the country, communally owned and operated by small groups of neighbors. The advantages of buying a dish were obvious—there were no fees to pay to any cable systems, no cable at all, and an unlimited choice of programming from all over the world. The drawback was that everyone had to tune in to the same thing. The dish controversy would prove to be an annoying one, resolved by the FCC later in the season.

The season. In spite of all that had occurred, America was returning home from summer vacation and getting ready for the fall spectacle of new shows. Three questions formed part of the annual rites of TV, three questions that were asked every September and forgotten by October: how much money would Jerry Lewis raise, what shows would win Emmies, and, most important, who would become Miss America?

4 Preseason Rituals: The Jerry Lewis Telethon, The Emmies, Miss America

This television season began like the others before it, steeped in ritual and repetition. Three live (and therefore uniquely television) shows coming one after another signal the official start of the new season. The first of these shows is "The Jerry Lewis Telethon." In a medium intent on retreating from the ambivalence of live broadcasting to the safety of film and videotape, the telethon remains one of the few traditions surviving from the early days of small-room television. Hosted by Jerry Lewis, the TV fund-raiser was a natural extension of the real-life morality plays of summer 1981. Effectively underscoring the flailings of the TV preachers, Lewis is a master of audience manipulation for the purpose of contribution. Pay, you healthy sinners, pay! Through the years, Lewis has become ever more zealous in his demands. Perhaps his dystrophic gestures have something to do with his own motivations, or the guilt remaining from his role as Jewish boychik to the Italian lover-boy Dean Martin. The success of the comic duo, after a one-hundred-dollar appearance on the first "Ed Sullivan Show," catapulted the team to superstardom. The first series of New York-based muscular dystrophy telethons were, in fact, hosted by Dean Martin and Jerry Lewis. When Martin decided to throw in the towel, Lewis agreed to continue to host the show, thereby turning the annual plea into an annual event. The "Muscular Dystrophy Telethon" soon became "The Jerry Lewis Telethon for Muscular Dystrophy." Every Labor Day weekend, Jerry can be counted on to promenade his stuff for twenty-two hours. He is hero and martyr, not sleeping, not eating, loosening his tie and rolling up his sleeves, manipulating his viewers through sympathy and guilt, parading victims and benefactors alternately throughout the night and day.

Each year a telethon must be a greater success, financially, than the previous year, or, in spite of how much money is raised, we know it isn't a success at all. Telethons begin with a flourish of big-name entertainment strategically placed to capture the largest audiences at any given time. Frank Sinatra is always booked for the best hours, surrounded by "tote boards," loose ties, sweat, shouting, tears, patriotism, and money, money, money. With Lewis, though, there is only one real star, and that's Jerry. A giant TV screen behind him reminds us in case we miss the point, a larger than life, visual echo.

In true live-TV fashion, the 1981 telethon began in total disarray. It didn't begin at all in the East. Most affiliates (nearly all that carried the show on the East Coast) were reluctant to cut away from an NFL game—Houston versus Los Angeles—because they remembered the debacle of 1968, known unaffectionately on TV Row as "the Heidi Affair." That year, NBC cut away from a Jets game with the Jets two touchdowns ahead. Confident of Namath's arm, the network pulled out of the game and went into "Heidi." This demonstration of format before content backfired. Oakland, the Jets' opponent, scored three touchdowns in the final seconds, one of the greatest comebacks never seen in the Jets' hometown, New York City, and the rest of the East Coast.

Telethon or no telethon, the switch for the one-time affiliate hook-up wasn't thrown until the football game ended (Houston 27, Los Angeles 20). Once on the air, the show was plagued with audio problems, much to the chagrin and rage of self-styled technical whiz Jerry. Things weren't all right until Wayne Newton officially got things going by sweating himself nearly to death during his rendition of "The Impossible Dream." Lewis followed, telling his audience that he never goes to supermarkets anymore, before bringing on the representative of General Foods, there to make a giant contribution. Sinatra appeared at 11:00 EST, via closed-circuit hook-up from Atlantic City, New Jersey, where he sang "New York, New York." Again the sound system faltered. Someone forgot to make up Frankie's hands for color TV, and they showed up pearly white as the camera came in for close-ups of the Chairman of the Board holding the mike. This was followed by a surprise appearance from Tony Orlando, who'd been out, he told us, collecting money door-to-door.

The show hit the one-million-dollar mark in seventy-two minutes. Lewis would raise thirty-two million dollars in twenty hours—the most successful "Jerry Lewis Telethon" to date—while the government was still trying, after nine months, to pass a budget through Congress.

A week after the telethon came the thirty-third annual presentation of the Emmy Awards, television's pat on its own back. Award shows tend to proliferate on television, although no one really cares who wins or who loses. It's more a question of who's with whom, who's wearing what, and watching live television giving away something of value. In this sense, award shows are like quiz shows: prizes for the winners, too-bads for the losers. The action at the Emmies is seeing Alan Alda clean shaven and in civvies, hearing Carroll O'Connor speak without a Queens accent, and trying to see who Victoria Principal is with. Can you remember the show that won best program of 1975? The best performance by an actress last year? This year?

The 1981 Emmies were hosted by Ed Asner and Shirley MacLaine. Asner's appearance was seen as a victory of sorts for the Screen Actors Guild, and, in retrospect, the kickoff to his December bid for the union's presidency. In the preceding year, during the height of the SAG strike, Asner organized the boycott of the Emmy broadcast. The only actor who crossed the picket line to accept his award for best performance in 1980 was James Boothe, who won for his portrayal of Jim Jones in a TV docudrama of the last days of the mass-suicide ritual in Guyana. Has anyone heard from Boothe since?

If Asner was intent on making his presence as a heavyweight felt, the show still had its inevitable live-TV moments. There was Nancy Marchand talking seriously about the stroke suffered by Mrs. Pynchon, the character Marchand portrays on "Lou Grant," followed almost immediately by Shirley MacLaine ad-libbing, on an unrelated subject, "Well, different strokes for different folks!"

And the clips. Always the clips. Once more we saw Ethel Merman, Mary Martin, Judy Garland, Frank Sinatra, and Fred Astaire. None, of course, known primarily as a television performer nor particularly successful on the tube. More of an embarassment than an accolade, Emmy montages remind us of how few the memorable moments really are, and worse, how little those doing the picking know about television's history.

There was one memorable moment at the 1981 Emmies: the appearance of Rod Steiger, on hand to give a reading in honor of the recent passing of Paddy Chayefsky. Steiger was introduced by Peter O'Toole, graceful and much the guest of the Academy. When Steiger took over, doing the "mad as hell" speech from *Network,* the hall vibrated with emotion. Steiger's neck-bulging performance should have been nominated for an Emmy. Of all the Chayefsky material available, including the plays originally done on television—*Marty,* for one—the choice of the award-winning feature movie *Network,* a scathing indictment of media manipulation and behind-the-scenes tactics in big-time TV, was fascinating, perhaps one more "purge" session, this one held in public.

The little moments. The opening credits showed Bruce Jenner as the star of "CHiPs," a part he never played. Ella Fitzgerald was not able to read cue cards, a problem with presenters since the early days of television. Why presenters at awards can't memorize thirty seconds worth of material remains as big a mystery as why they can't read cue cards.

And, of course, the smallest, most forgettable moments of all. The awards themselves.

"Hill Street Blues" swept the Emmies. The show took eight statuettes. "Hill Street" was Fred Silverman's last hurrah, produced by Grant Tinker, his successor. For the record, here is the list of the major award winners:

Drama Series—"Hill Street Blues."
Comedy Series—"Taxi."
Variety, Music or Comedy Program—"Lily: Sold Out."
Drama Special—"Playing for Time."
Limited Series—"Shogun."
Actor in a Drama Series—Daniel Travanti for "Hill Street Blues."
Actress in a Drama Series—Barbara Babcock for "Hill Street Blues": "Fecund Hand Rose."

Actor in a Limited Series or Special—Anthony Hopkins for "The Bunker."

Actress in a Limited Series or Special—Vanessa Redgrave for "Playing for Time."

Actor in a Comedy Series—Judd Hirsch for "Taxi."

Actress in a Comedy Series—Isabel Sanford for "The Jeffersons."

Supporting Actor in a Comedy Series—Danny De Vito for "Taxi."

Supporting Actress in a Comedy Series—Eileen Brennan for "Private Benjamin."

Supporting Actor in a Drama Series—Michael Conrad of "Hill Street Blues."

Supporting Actress in a Drama Series—Nancy Marchand of "Lou Grant."

Supporting Actor in a Limited Series or Special —David Warner of "Masada."

Supporting Actress in a Limited Series or Special —Jane Alexander of "Playing for Time."

The third, and prettiest, leg of the start of the new season is the venerable Miss America pageant. This asexual absurdity, long a staple of high ratings, began to slip two years ago. The producers figured that the reason had to be the one host, not the fifty, count-em fifty, beautiful women. So they fired Bert Parks, in the dead of winter, hoping that no one would notice. The country reacted as if Santa Claus had been found frozen to death. The story reached a certain dubious importance when it became a part of Johnny's nightly monologue on "The Tonight Show." Only Alexander Haig has since attained that high a distinction. The backlash against firing Parks should have been obvious to the producers of the Miss America pageant. Demographically, the show's largest audience is the over-fifty crowd. This is not to imply that the producers weren't aware of their audience—just the opposite.

People over fifty haven't got as much money as the under-twenty-five crowd to spend on commercial products. They have barely enough money to pay for the electricity needed to keep their TV sets running. However, replacing Bert Parks with Ron Ely, whose chief claim to fame was that he played Tarzan, a role not associated with great charm, was a further step in the wrong direction. The obvious move was to choose a woman as the host.

The first post-Parks "Miss America," starring Ron Ely, dropped 10 percent in the ratings. Bye-bye Ely. Albert Marks, Jr., pageant chairman, announced: "We've embarked on a policy of changing personalities as we think expedient. . . . Ron Ely stepped into a tough job."

Ely was replaced by Gary Collins, whose comment to the press was meant to heal all wounds: "I'm not sure I'll be asked to sing 'There She Is . . .' but I'm willing to." Collins' credentials included the fact that he was married to a former Miss America. Which former Miss America? Who can tell one Miss America from another? Who cares? It's really not important which Miss America wins, just as long she cries a little, almost drops the tiara, speaks with a strong regional accent, and isn't an obvious lesbian Communist.

The Telethon, the Emmies, and "Miss America" share a stylistic aspect that acknowledges the early days of television. Once the ritual passes, though, it's down to business, with new shows that are slicker, quicker, and more contemporary than the year before. If they're void of real drama, excitement, or conflict, that's okay too. Quick cutting can create kinetic suspense. Car crashes can pass for action. Titillation is easier than sensuality. With the strike interrupting production, the introduction of the season's new shows was necessarily staggered. When the curtain finally went up, the effects of all that had happened behind the scenes were about to be seen full-front.

Here, in descending order, is a list of the most popular summer shows of 1981. America tuned in to a mixed bag of holdover series, canceled show reruns, made-for-TV movies, pilot shows that didn't make it, and a couple of odd summertime specials. The period covered is April 20 to October 4, 1981.

Rank	Title
1.	"Private Benjamin" (CBS)
2.	"The Two of Us" (CBS)
3.	"Nurse" (CBS)
4.	"Magnum, P.I." (CBS)
5.	"It's a Living" (ABC)
6.	"Checking In" (CBS)
7.	"ABC Monday" Movie
8.	"WKRP in Cincinnati" (CBS)
9.	"Tim Conway" (CBS)
10.	"ABC Summer Movie" (Wednesday)
11.	"American Dream" (ABC)
	"Vega$" (ABC)
13.	"Park Place" (CBS)
14.	"Hill Street Blues" (Tuesday) (NBC)
	"CBS Saturday Movies"
16.	"ABC's Monday Night Baseball"
17.	"Flamingo Road" (NBC)
18.	"Dynasty" (ABC)
19.	"Walter Cronkite's Universe" (CBS)
20.	"NBC Magazine"
	"Nero Wolfe" (Tuesday) (NBC)
22.	"ABC Comedy Special" (Monday)
	"Charlie's Angels" (ABC)
24.	"ABC Theater for Young Americans"
25.	"Walking Tall" (NBC)
26.	"NBC Comedy Theater"
	"The Krypton Factor" (ABC)
28.	"NBC Friday Night at the Movies"
	"Enos" (CBS)
	"Marie" (NBC)

Rank	Title
31.	"240-Robert" (ABC)
32.	"Steve Allen Comedy Hour" (NBC)
33.	"The Gangster Chronicles" (NBC)
	"NBC Saturday Night at the Movies"
	"Breaking Away" (ABC)
36.	"BJ and the Bear" (NBC)
37.	"Foul Play" (ABC)
38.	"Flo" (CBS)
39.	"The White Shadow" (CBS)
40.	"Sanford" (NBC)
	"Games People Play" (NBC)

The fall network schedule of programs
for the 1981–1982 TV season.

		8 P.M.	8:30 P.M.	9 P.M.	9:30 P.M.	10 P.M.	10:30 P.M.
Sunday	ABC	Today's FBI		ABC Sunday Night Movie			
	CBS	Archie Bunker's Place	One Day at a Time	Alice	Jeffersons	Trapper John, M.D.	
	NBC	CHiPs		NBC Sunday Night at the Movies			
Monday	ABC	That's Incredible		NFL Monday Night Football			
	CBS	Private Benjamin	Two of Us	M*A*S*H	House Calls	Lou Grant	
	NBC	Little House on the Prairie		NBC Monday Night at the Movies			
Tuesday	ABC	Happy Days	Laverne & Shirley	Three's Company	Too Close for Comfort	Hart to Hart	
	CBS	Simon & Simon		CBS Tuesday Night Movie			
	NBC	Father Murphy		Bret Maverick		Flamingo Road	
Wednesday	ABC	Greatest American Hero		The Fall Guy		Dynasty	
	CBS	Mr. Merlin	WKRP in Cincinnati	Nurse		Shannon	
	NBC	Real People		The Facts of Life	Love, Sidney	Quincy	
Thursday	ABC	Mork & Mindy	Best of the West	Barney Miller	Taxi	20/20	
	CBS	Magnum, P.I.		Knots Landing		Jessica Novak	
	NBC	Harper Valley	Lewis and Clark	Diff'rent Strokes	Gimme a Break	Hill Street Blues	
Friday	ABC	Benson	Open All Night	Maggie	Making a Living	Strike Force	
	CBS	Dukes of Hazzard		Dallas		Falcon Crest	
	NBC	NBC Magazine		McClain's Law		The Devlin Connection	
Saturday	ABC	King's Crossing		Love Boat		Fantasy Island	
	CBS	Walt Disney		CBS Saturday Night Movies			
	NBC	Barbara Mandrell		Nashville Palace		The Angie Dickinson Show	
		New Programs					

5 The Season

No sooner had Miss America wiped away her tears than the Reverend Wildmon declared his intention of organizing another boycott of advertisers of television shows deemed "unfit" by The Coalition for Better Television. And no sooner did the announcement gain headlines when it was called off. "A combination of factors" was cited by Wildmon, who warned, nevertheless, that the names of those companies that had been slated for boycott would be published in the coalition's monthly newsletter. "We are in a monitoring process," he announced. *Newsweek* published a picture of Wildmon sitting intently in front of a television set, pencil in hand, actually "monitoring." What was the coalition specifically looking out for? "Sexual content, violence content, profanity, and beverage consumption in programs," as well as sex-oriented commercials. Each show received an overall rating of 1 to 10 on a "constructive rating" scale, to be listed along with the sponsors of the shows. However, as the Reverend insisted, there was no boycott.

Because of the delay caused by the writers' strike, the start of the new season was a stutter-step affair. New shows replaced old ones when new episodes were ready. CBS and ABC announced the week of October 5 as their premiere week. NBC declined to declare, announcing that "last season we announced the start of the season in September and no one listened to us. This year we'll wait for our first night of high ratings and say it starts there."

Here is a breakdown of the new shows for the 1981–1982 season:

ABC:

Strike Force.
Starring Robert Stack. Action-adventure. Reminiscent of "The Untouchables."

Today's FBI.
Starring Mike Connors, formerly of "Mannix" and "Tightrope," taking over the Efrem Zimbalist, Jr., role from the original FBI series.

Open All Night.
Situation comedy in an all-night grocery store. Starring George Dzundza, a newcomer not unlike Carroll O'Connor's Archie Bunker.

Best of the West
A spoof of TV westerns. Starring Joel Higgins, Leonard Frey.

CBS:

Shannon.
Starring Kevin Dobson, formerly of "Kojak." A New York detective transferred to San Francisco. Interesting twist: the death of his wife had made him impotent.

Simon and Simon.
Countrified male bonding. Rumor had it that this show's scripts underwent close, specific scrutiny from the Moral Majority before going into production.

Jessica Novak.
The story of a woman news-reporter and her attempts at covering stories not confined to women. Derivative of a couple of Jane Fonda movies.

NBC:

McClain's Law.
Starring James Arness. A cop comes out of retirement.

The Devlin Connection.
Starring Rock Hudson. A cop comes out of retirement.

Bret Maverick.
Starring James Garner. Maverick comes out of retirement.

("The Devlin Connection" was postponed one full season due to Rock Hudson's unexpected ill health and open heart surgery. "Bret Maverick" was shut down for a while when James Garner hurt himself falling off a mechanical horse.)

Love, Sidney.
Starring Tony Randall. A gay middle-aged man cares for an actress's fatherless daughter. Situation comedy.

Father Murphy.
Starring Merlin Olsen. A spinoff of the network's most popular and successful series, "Little House on the Prairie."

Gimme a Break.
Starring Nell Carter and Dolph Sweet. Domestic situation comedy.

The Powers of Matthew Starr.
Starring Peter Barton. A prince from another planet
enrolls in high school. A "Mork and Mindy" clone.

ABC, which had always been the network with the
shortest skirts, tightest blouses, and prettiest faces, was
playing it very safe: established stars, one revamped pro-
government detective series, an innocuous sit-com, and a
light spoof. CBS, the ratings leader the past two seasons,
made the least number of changes on its schedule. NBC,
on the other hand, unable to shed the dubious distinction
of being the "third network," juggled its schedule as
much as possible, relying heavily on well-known stars
(Garner, Hudson, Arness, Randall) to reclaim lost ratings
territory. The switch from Silverman to Tinker also
brought transitional problems. Tinker promoted Brandon
Tartikoff to head of programming. Tartikoff—young, aggressive, and corporation to the core—started rejecting
Silverman projects as soon as possible. Angie Dickinson's new series, produced by Carson Productions, was
"delayed." "The Chicago Story," another Silverman go,
was rejected, even though NBC, relying more than the
other networks on new product, was still caught short
because of the strike. Premiere week at ABC and CBS
took place while NBC continued to run episodes of such
has-been and never-were series as "Here's Boomer,"
"Fitz and Bones," and "The Flintstones."

One new network trend is the debuting of a
"major" miniseries to kick off the new season. The miniseries is usually aimed at a particular ethnic group, a
precedent set when "Roots" proved to be the ratings
smash of 1977. "Roots" begat "Shogun," "Shogun" begat
"Masada," and "Masada" begat this season's offering,
"The Manions." Nineteen eighty-one was the Year of the
Irish on ABC.

"The Manions" began, as they all do, with a birth, lots

of old-country in the background, lots of running, riding, shouting, calling. "The Manions" sported a host of big name celebrities in cameo roles, in the same manner as "Roots." Big names, big ratings. However, the story of one family's survival during the Great Potato Famine of 1845 turned out to be about as dramatic as McDonald's running out of french fries.

Over at NBC, "McClain's Law" (starring James Arness) managed to make it to the air. James Arness was a proven star with a twenty-year run in "Gunsmoke." Arness had a very high "Q" rating. A Q measures a personality's popularity and appeal, regardless of what role he or she is playing.* A high Q can mean the difference between early cancellation and a second chance, maybe a schedule change to a different night, in an effort to save a series. Although it never made a serious dent in the ratings, "McClain's Law" hung in for the entire season, first on Friday night, then on Saturday night. The show was slotted Fridays against "Dallas," the number-one show in the ratings the past two seasons. It was hoped that Arness would be able to take some audience away from J.R. "McClain's Law" was a show built around Arness's Q. What was needed was a format that would work for the aging, limping actor, whose leathery face and snow-white hair were a far cry from the visage of the heroic Matt Dillon of the early "Gunsmoke." Arness's broad shoulders and narrow waist seemed somehow to have changed places. The first episode dealt with an ex-cop who decides to become "unretired" so that he can personally avenge the murder of a friend. To broaden the show's appeal, Arness was given a young, blond partner. To insure no trouble with excessive "jiggling," his partner was a young, blond man. Added in were a running "feud" with the

---

*Officially, the networks claim not to use the "Q" rating. However, several network executives I interviewed told me, off the record, that everyone respects the power of the "Q."

D.A. for a touch of humor, and an emphasis on conservative wisdom.

If "McClain's Law" seemed reminscent of "Barnaby
Jones," the similarity probably wasn't all that uninten-
tional. CBS's "Barnaby Jones," starring the highly Q'd
Buddy Ebsen (of "The Beverly Hillbillies" fame, and before that the "Davy Crockett" Disney trilogy of the fifties
that made coonskin caps a national craze), had lasted for
years, requiring very little from Ebsen besides visibility.
If Ebsen looked a little silly taking on bad guys who were
forty years his junior, no problem. CBS eliminated virtually all violence from "Jones," much to the pleasure of
those concerned with excessive violence on TV.

As for "McClain," they dressed Arness in contemporary cords, neat shirts, snappy colors, and white shoes.
And they left the rear-view mirror off his patrol car. No
use looking back.

CBS, the ratings leader, had virtually no live programming left on its schedule. "Dallas" continued to
dominate, while made-for-TV movies emphasized the vir-
tue of those who worked in the military, or as police, or
as agents of one kind or another.

Back on ABC, "Today's FBI" was less interested in
political subversives this time around and more involved
in fighting organized crime. The premiere-week episode
outdrew "Archie Bunker's Place" (CBS), a long-standing
ratings winner. This was due, at least in part, to Mike
Connors' very high Q rating. Personable, soft-spoken,
well-liked in the industry as well as by the public, Connors
was an excellent choice to promote the image of the new,
modern FBI. Side-kicking with Connors was a black agent
recruited from "Intelligence." A sexually provocative female psychologist and weapons expert rounded out the
series regulars. In real life, "today's" FBI has 7,760 agents:
all are white males except for 351 women and 237 blacks
and hispanics.

One interesting twist in "Today's FBI" was a subplot

in which Agent Connors' wife was constantly complaining about his work which kept him away for long stretches. This is the situation that the network felt American women could identify with: not that another woman might steal her husband away (remember that weapons expert), but that the dinner might get burned.

Another revival of sorts was NBC's "Saturday Night Live," part three. After five years of inventive, intelligent, cruel, incisive, excessive, riotous, and regrettable moments, the kids with the sharp street instincts who went for the jugular deserted the show. By 1980, "Saturday Night Live" had also lost its producer and apparently its guts. The second-generation cast huffed and puffed through one disastrous season, climaxing in a suicidal "Fuck You!" screamed by one member, smiling, into the faces of America. During "Saturday Night Live's" heyday, NBC owned the 11:30–1:00 weekend timeslot. For a while ABC offered youth-oriented movies opposite "Live," but endless reruns of Jack Nicholson motorcycle movies or Kris Kristofferson zombielike in drenched drug films just didn't do the trick.

For 1981, NBC faced a familiar problem. How was it going to keep a hit show on the air without the people who made it a hit in the first place? It happens often in TV: those responsible for a hit show, particularly the writers, frequently are promoted to the next level of production or move on to a new show.

With 1980–1981 producer Jean Doumanian fired, NBC recalled "Saturday Night Live's" original producer, Dick Ebersol, to perform miracle surgery in a last-ditch effort to save the show. An entire new cast was hired. By October 1981, the revamped "Saturday Night Live" hit the airwaves.

The funniest show of the 1981–1982 season was "Second City," otherwise known as "SCTV Network," aired

Friday nights on NBC at 12:30 EST. Relentlessly, "SCTV" delivered the best, most accurate satire of television itself, something at which the original "Saturday Night Live" cast had been so expert. Awesome takeoffs of TV "legends" Bob Hope, Walter Cronkite, Perry Como, Joey Heatherton, Liza Minnelli, and Merv Griffin, combined with the mythical "stars" of "SCTV's" own "network" brought out the true meaning of ensemble performing. Not since the days of Sid Caeser and Imogene Coca had television witnessed such a highly sustained level of performing. The comic talents of John Candy, Joe Flaherty, Rick Moranis, Dave Thomas, Catherine O'Hara, and Andrea Martin exposed the hollowness of an Orson Welles doing commercials for wine, Bob Hope relentlessly plugging another special, or a Merv Griffin too complacent to turn his body when his head spins around during one of his endless gossip-saturated talk show installments.

NBC, the "third network," had the two funniest shows of the season. So what did they do with them? They put them on late-night schedules, off prime time. But at least they put them on.

6 The Ratings—I

The first "week" of the new season had begun. Actually, the debuts were staggered, but enough of the new prime-time shows were aired, and the first significant ratings sheet for the new season was out. Here's the way it looked for the week ending October 4.

SHOW	NETWORK	RATING/SHARE
1. "Hart to Hart" (R)	ABC	23.5/39
2. "Three's Company" (R)	ABC	23.1/37
3. "The Jeffersons"	CBS	22.4/34
4. "The Dukes of Hazzard" (R)	CBS	22.2/38
5. "M*A*S*H" (R)	CBS	22.1/33
6. "Monday Night Football"	ABC	22.0/37
7. "Alice"	CBS	21.9/33
8. "60 Minutes"	CBS	20.5/36
9. "Trapper John, M.D."	CBS	20.3/33
10. "House Calls" (R)	CBS	20.1/31
11. "Laverne and Shirley" (R)	ABC	20.0/32
12. "Dallas" (R)	CBS	19.9/36

	SHOW	NETWORK	RATING SHARE
13.	"Real People"	NBC	19.3/32
14.	"Diff'rent Strokes" (R)	NBC	18.7/30
15.	"The Manions of America (part 1)	ABC	18.5/31

Network averages   ABC: 17.3   CBS: 16.9   NBC: 13.8

The first week went to ABC, slightly ahead of CBS, with NBC way back behind them both. A closer examination of this first week reveals some interesting facts. First, with the exception of "Monday Night Football" and the first episode of "The Manions of America," ABC won the ratings battle with reruns, whereas CBS ran new episodes of "The Jeffersons," "Alice," "60 Minutes" (only one episode was new—the other two were repeats), and "Trapper John, M.D." NBC placed only one show in the national top fifteen, "Diff'rent Strokes," a repeat episode. Eight shows out of the top fifteen were situation comedies; four out of the first five, five out of the first seven. The first episode of "The Manions of America" edged into the final spot at the bottom of the top fifteen, with its second and third episodes placing out of the money.

"Hart to Hart," the top-rated show of the first week of the new season, was up against a Tuesday Night CBS Movie and NBC's popular "Dallas"-type "Flamingo Road," an evening soap opera. "Alice," "The Jeffersons," and "Trapper John" formed a solid block of Sunday CBS domination against "CHiPs" (a one-time ratings winner, fading fast) and an NBC movie, while ABC also threw in a movie in self-defense. Most notable in the listing, however, is that of all the regularly scheduled new series— "Today's FBI," "Simon and Simon," "Father Murphy," "Bret Maverick," "The Fall Guy," "Shannon," "Love, Sidney," "Best of the West," "Jessica Novack," "Lewis and Clark," "Gimme a Break," Open All Night," "Maggie,"

"Strike Force," "Falcon Crest," "NBC Magazine," "McClain's Law," "The Devlin Connection," "King's Crossing," and "Nashville Palace"—not one placed in the top fifteen.

How do the ratings work and what do the numbers mean? There are two major ratings services, A.C. Nielsen and Arbitron. For general computation, the Nielsens, as they are known, are recorded and published for the networks, which pay for this service.

The Nielsen system works on a random viewer monitoring system, based on 1,200 homes in which the family television is augmented with tallying equipment. These "audimeters" tell the Nielson Company two important facts: first, how many sets are tuned to a particular program at any given time and, second, how many sets are in use, turned on, regardless of what is being viewed. The first figure is known as the "rating" point, the second the "share." Nielsen estimates that each TV household in America represents an average of two viewers, or approximately 1.5 million people per rating point in 1980. In the ratings listed above for the first week of the new season, the second number in the last column is the share. The generally accepted minimum for a program is a 15 rating and, a 30 share. Of the 39 percent of all TV sets in America that were turned on during "Hart to Hart," for example, 23.5 percent of those viewers were watching the popular action-comedy series during the week of October 4.

What's the difference—a rating point here, a rating point there, a couple of hundred viewers here, a few more there? Remember those figures about how much a minute of advertising cost on a top-rated network television program? "Dallas," you'll recall, was able to snag

$175,000 for a thirty-second spot, $350,000 for one minute. Consider that a program on prime time has almost sixteen minutes of advertising space available, and you can begin to see where the big dollars come from. The amount a network can charge for space on a television show is determined by how many people a sponsor of a show can reach. Think of it in terms of subscriptions to magazines. Publications will offer gigantic savings if you subscribe to them because all magazines that carry advertising work off rate sheets, and a subscription list guarantees a certain number of issues being printed. The number of sales over the counter is gravy, and can be used in retrospect, but it's the subscriptions that set the price of ads. On television, ratings numbers are where the action is.

Further, it costs upwards of $200,000 for a producer to produce a one-hour episode of a major television program (projections based on 1982 figures make this number conservative). Since producers lease their programs to the networks, it would seem that all that's necessary is to make a show for less money than the millions made from an episode. However, that's not the way it works. Producers usually lose money on the shows they produce.

A producer leases a series to a network usually for a first run and first rerun, under a licensing agreement. Naturally, it is in the network's interest to pay as little as possible for the show and charge as much as possible for commercial space. It is in the producer's interest to charge as much as possible for the leasing of his program, but not so much that the program will be unprofitable for the network, which, in addition to licensing fees, must build in promotional costs and run the risk of early cancellation—resulting in a stockpile of leased, but never shown, episodes. Producers, on the other hand, must go ahead and produce episodes, weeks in advance, stockpiling on the same risk that their shows may never get on the air, thus hurting their future relationship with the networks and possibly the life of their production company.

The classic example of a producer with a show so successful he nearly went "broke" is Norman Lear, who jumped the gun on syndication with "All in the Family," selling the rights to a syndication firm during the heyday of "Family's" prime-time run. This occurred in the mid-seventies, when Lear had "Mary Hartman, Mary Hartman," "Alice," "All in the Family," "The Jeffersons," and other shows running in prime time. One of the standard jokes in the industry was that if he were any more successful, he'd go broke, because his production costs always ran higher than his first-run licensing fees. By putting "All in the Family" into syndicated reruns while the show was still hot in first run, he broke a cardinal rule of television: never go into competition with yourself. The prevalent thinking before "All in the Family" went into reruns was that syndicating a show still in prime time would kill its first-run appeal. Why bother to watch it Saturday night when it's on every day of the week? But Lear proved the fallacy of prevailing television logic, just as he had by bringing "All in the Family" to American TV in the first place (with the significant aid of Fred Silverman). It was a show that no network had the courage to put on the air when it was first conceived. Following Lear's syndication coup, all the top-rated shows began popping up off prime time, everything from "M*A*S*H" to "Dallas" doing daily duty while sustaining popularity in first run.

Who produces television shows? The answer to this question is more complex than one might imagine. It's not a world of mythic overnight success. Television is basically a closed shop, still operating for all intents and purposes with a variation of the notorious "blacklist," or what is now referred to in the industry as the "approval list." A director, for example, will not work in television if he or she is not on a network "approval list." Neither will an actor or a producer. Denials and defenses abound, but my first-hand experience says otherwise. The initial consideration by the producers of the first major television network special I wrote—before a word had been typed by my itchy fingers—was whether I could be "approved."

One production company which is highly approved and highly successful in television is Lorimar Productions. Lorimar currently produces "Dallas," "Flamingo Road," "Knots Landing," and "Falcon Crest," all prime-time winners. What follows is a list of their most successful TV series and miniseries now offered for syndication:

TV SERIES

The Waltons
Apple's Way
Doc Elliot
The Blue Knight
Hunter
Eight Is Enought
Dallas
The Young Pioneers
The Waverly Wonders
Kaz
Flatbush
Married: The First Year
Big Shamus, Little Shamus
Knots Landing
Skag
Flamingo Road
Secrets of Midland Heights

MOVIES OF THE WEEK

Girls of Huntington House
Don't Be Afraid of the
  Dark
Dream for Christmas
Dying Room Only
Stranger Within
The Runaways
Conspiracy of Terror
The Runaway Barge
Returning Home
Eric
Widow
Prince of Central Park
Green Eyes
Bad Ronald
A Question of Guilt
Desperate Women
The Long Journey Back
Some Kind of Miracle
Young Love, First Love
Marriage Is Alive & Well in
  the U.S.A.
Mary and Joseph:
  A Story of Faith
A Perfect Match
Rape and Marriage:
  The Rideout Case
A Matter of Life and Death

MINISERIES

The Blue Knight	Mr. Horn
Sybil	Studs Lonigan
Helter Skelter	A Man Called Intrepid

Now, let's take a look at Lorimar's complete list of available shows. An industry rule of thumb is that a show is sellable if it can be summed up in a sentence, is not controversial, sounds like every other show of the same genre, and has potential across-the-ratings-board potential. In other words, mom and dad can sit through it along with big-bucks Teenage Billy. Teenage Billy, you might be interested to know, has been designated as the biggest potential spender-purchaser, with Housewife Hannah coming in second, Middle-age Mary following in the show place, and Dreary Dad good only for tires and beer on the weekends.

You'll notice in the list that there are a few shows that you may have never heard of. These are shows that never made it to air and are now "bargains" for syndication. "Moose," one half-hour NBC comedy pilot that never aired, becomes a highly commercial project for those late August and early September "dead" weeks when ratings demographics reveal that no one is watching television anyway.* Air has to be filled. Further, "Moose" might score big in the ratings, and suddenly a network executive might decide that it is perfect for the "second season," the crop of replacement shows that usually come in bunches around January, after the first "sweep" ratings have been fully analyzed. "Sweeps" are one-month periods when the Nielsens are most highly focused. They come three times a year, in months considered to be prime for television viewing (November, February, and May).

---

*"Moose" finally aired briefly during the summer of 1982.

"The Waltons"
The story of a large family living in the Blue Ridge Mountains of Virginia during the Depression.

"Apple's Way"
A contemporary family moves from Los Angeles to Iowa to lead a simpler, healthier life.

"Doc Elliot"
A city doctor moves to a rural area of Colorado to practice medicine.

"Girls of Huntington House"
Girls, young, unmarried, and pregnant and for the most part frightened half to death, come to Huntington House to get help through a very difficult period of time.

"Don't Be Afraid of the Dark"
Alex and Sandy Farnham inherit an old house and the haunting voices in the dark that go with it.

"Dream for Christmas"
Reverend Will Douglas and his family leave their secure and familiar home in Arkansas for a more rewarding and challenging position in California.

"Dying Room Only"
Jean Mitchell comes out of the ladies room in a rundown cafe in the middle of the desert to find her husband Bob missing and no help from anyone to find him.

"Stranger Within"
When Ann Collins learns that she's pregnant even though her husband had a vasectomy and she's been with no other man, a friend suggests she may be pregnant by an extraterrestrial being.

"The Runaways"
A young boy runs away from his foster home and meets up with Yarra, a grown leopard who has escaped from the zoo.

"Conspiracy of Terror"
A Jewish husband and gentile wife detective team work in the suburbs and uncover a religious cult that worships the devil.

"The Runaway Barge"
The adventures of two young men who work on the boat The River King on the Mississippi River.

"Returning Home"
The story of three men returning to their respective homes after serving in World War II and the problems they have adjusting to their families and civilian life.

"The Blue Knight"
"The Blue Knight" is about the life and adventures of Bumper Morgan, a colorful old-timer in the police force who patrols his beat on foot.

"Eric"
The story of a strong college athlete who is stricken at the age of eighteen by a terminal illness.

"Widow"
A young woman learns to cope with the world and raise her children without a father after her husband dies of cancer.

"Where's Momma?"
Lina Sprague has recently died and her husband Harry has been trying to manage by himself to take care of their twin sons until Lina comes back in a mystical form so that only Harry can see or speak to her.

"Moose"
It is 1950 and Moose, a high school senior on a bet with his buddy, tries to make his fantasy a reality when he asks his art teacher for a date.

"Pomroy's People"
Reverend Russell Pomroy and his people, the residents of the small, backwards town of Blue Creek, work together when things get tough.

"Prince of Central Park"
An eleven-year-old boy and his younger sister run away from their foster home and experience many adventures in their new dwelling—a treehouse in Central Park, New York City.

"Helter Skelter"
Based on Vincent Bugliosi's book *Helter Skelter*. It is the story of Charles Manson and family and the brutal Tate/La Bianca murders.

"Green Eyes"
A black American soldier returns to Viet Nam after the war to search for his child in the overflowing Vietnamese orphanages.

"Bad Ronald"
Ronald Wilby slowly goes crazy when his mother hides him in a secret area of their home after he accidentally kills a neighborhood girl and then his mother dies on an operating table and he's left alone in the world.

"You're Just Like Your Father"
A New York hustler lives with his son and daughter-in-law, whom he is always trying to con into his schemes.

"People Like Us"
The story of the Allmans, who are a blue-collar family, and the events that revolve around their trying to make ends meet.

"Eight Is Enough"
The story, based on the book by Thomas Braden, of the Bradfords who have eight children with contemporary problems.

"Marriage & Other Flights of Fancy"
David Bradford and his friend Linda take off on the road in his Bronco to find themselves.

"Making It"
A story of four pre-law students who live in an apartment together.

"Sybil"
Based on the book by Flora Rheta Schreiber. It is the true story of a girl with sixteen personalities and how her psychiatrist treated her for this unusual sickness.

"Bunco"
Ben Gordean and Ed Walker are a team on the Bunco Squad, fighting rackets and con games that come down.

"Bravo Two"
Bud Whizzer and Wiley Starrett patrol Marina del Rey aboard the Harbor Patrol boat, Bravo-Two.

"Last Chance"
Life at the Carver Creek Ranch for boys is a battle of wits between the boys in bunkhouse D and the camp establishment.

"Killer on Board"
An unknown killer disease breaks out aboard a luxury liner and nobody can get off until a cure is found.

"Hunter"
James Hunter and Marty Shaw are agents for a special secret government group taking on the things that the CIA and FBI cannot handle.

"The Wilds of Ten Thousand Islands"
The Wild family live on an island in Ten Thousand Islands, Florida, and take care of an experiment with animals.

"A Question of Guilt"

Doris Winter's kids are murdered and the police think she did it.

"The Young Pioneers"

The Beatons try to build a new life for themselves on the plains of the Dakota Territory.

"Dallas"

Power and sex are prominent in the Ewing family, who own a large cattle and oil ranch outside of Dallas.

"The Waverly Wonders"

Harry Casey, an ex-pro basketball player, comes to Waverly High to coach a team that has never won a game.

"Kaz"

Kaz is an ex-con who became a lawyer while in prison and uses his street savy to help him win cases.

"Flatbush"

The Flatbush Fungos are a group of five guys who help and also hinder the neighborhood in which they live.

"Married: The First Year"

The story of a young couple's first year of marriage.

"Desperate Women"

A U.S. Marshal finds three women prisoners and transports them across the desert.

"Mr. Horn"

The story of legendary gunfighter and Indian scout Tom Horn, his part in the capture of Geronimo, and his life in the American Southwest.

"Studs Lonigan"

The story of a young Irish boy and his struggle to grow up in Chicago from the early 1900s to the Depression.

"The Long Journey Back"
The story of a young girl's rehabilitation following a tragic accident in which she loses a leg

"Some Kind of Miracle"
The story of a young man's comeback after being paralyzed in a body-surfing accident.

"A Man Called Intrepid"
The story of Englishman William Stevenson and the people who helped break the German secret code during World War II.

"Me and Ducky"
The story of a teenage girl and her high school friends.

"Two Guys from Muck"
Buzz and Louie, a reporter and photographer, get stories for *Muck* magazine, a *National Enquirer*-type magazine.

"Knots Landing"
The story of Gary Ewing and his wife and three other families living in the same California cul-de-sac.

"Big Shamus, Little Shamus"
The story of Arnie, an old-time house detective, and his son Max and the changes in their lives when gambling comes to the Atlantic City hotel where they live.

"The Boss and the Secretary"
The story of a midwestern advertising executive transplanted to New York and his relationship with his kooky secretary.

"Young Love, First Love"
Teenagers dealing with their first loves

"Marriage Is Alive and Well in the U.S.A."
Four vignettes of married life tied together by a narrator

"Joshua's World"
A widower doctor fights bigotry in Arkansas in the 1930s.

"Reward"
A disillusioned cop turns bounty hunter to avenge the killing of his friend.

"Dusty"
Cab driver becomes an apprentice to a private eye.

"Flamingo Road"
Various residents of small northern Florida town.

"Cages"
A story of women in prison.

"Skag"
The story of a steelworker and his family.

"Mary and Joseph: A Story of Faith"
The young lives of the biblical couple, Mary and Joseph.

The advice the networks have for people trying to get into television is not to bring their ideas directly to them, but to try a production house, such as Lorimar. Lorimar is successful and powerful in the industry because, in addition to being able to repackage and refinance prime-time hits from other producers, it has the number-one show on television, "Dallas." This gives Lorimar a lot of leverage.

Still, being on the approval list, getting an idea past the pilot stage, getting the go-ahead for six episodes, making it onto a network schedule, and beating the ratings game is one of the most difficult, elusive objectives in the world of entertainment. There are so many people to deal with, and so few who are capable of making anything resembling a decision. One of the reasons the ratings have become such a powerful tool is that they are provided by independent services: something to blame for a show's failure, a place to point to when a show succeeds.

7 Drugs

Item: Gail Fisher of TV's "General Hospital," the most successful day-time soap opera, announced early in January that she was suing *TV Guide* magazine for one million dollars for claiming she used cocaine. The allegation was made in an article published in the popular television magazine, titled "It's Snowing in Hollywood Every Day."

Item: In the first week of the "new" season, NBC aired an antidrug jingle, "Get High on Yourself," every hour during prime-time broadcasting. The climax of the weekly campaign was a special featuring fifty-five sports and entertainment celebrities hosted by Bob Hope, in a concerted effort to combat the "growing drug problem in Hollywood." The campaign was produced by Bob Evans as part of his sentence for attempting to buy five ounces of cocaine for nineteen thousand dollars in New York the year before.

The question of drugs in Hollywood has been a double-edged sword for as long as the entertainment industry has been there. On the one hand, drugs have served as the theme for numerous movies, and have costarred in the real-life dramas of many Hollywood stars and celebrities. Drug use is part of the game, part of the flash of Beverly Hills status; it has always been so. On the other hand, the use of drugs has produced the greatest scandals in tinseltown history, linked to murders, rapes, and other acts of horror, from Fatty Arbuckle to John Belushi. Along with scandal has come a continuing cycle of vigilantism, the other edge of the sword. The more outrageous and widespread drug use in Hollywood has become, the more concentrated, organized, and effective have groups of civic-minded moralists become, with their boycotts, exposés and political and economic pressures on law enforcement operations to curb the use of illicit substances.

Drug use has been treated in a peculiar time warp in Hollywood films and television programs. In the sixties, at the height of marijuana use among college students, it became a staple of the music business, the "other" industry in Hollywood. Yet there wasn't a single film that dealt seriously with the subject. The most requested film on marijuana, particularly among the same college students who were its most devoted users, was *Reefer Madness*, a thirties propaganda movie in which a clean-cut youngster is driven to murder his girlfriend and sentenced to life imprisonment, all because he smoked a single joint of grass. Television finally felt ready to deal with the subject of marijuana in a dizzying 1968 "Dragnet" episode wherein Jack Webb made what amounted to a thirty-minute sermon on the mount and finally arrested a couple of whacked-out hippies who looked as if they were in search of the Manson Gang to invite over for a spot of tea. Of course, the psychedelic sixties was the decade of hallucinogens, LSD, psilocybin, and magic mushrooms, all of which were off limits to TV until well into the seventies. By this time all the spaced-out drugs were considered passé by the inner circle, now into cocaine. Not until the eighties was cocaine even acknowledged to exist on television. What the public wasn't aware of, though, was how much a part of the industry cocaine had become, or how much the public had been subsidizing the cocaine epidemic.

Take the story of "Jim" (not his real name), a friend of mine now working in Hollywood.

I first met Jim through a mutual friend in 1968 in New York, when I was living alone in my first apartment. Jim, just in from the Coast, where he'd been born and raised, wanted to be an actor. His first job in New York was the same as most actors—a waiter in an east-side singles bar. Spotted by a talent scout, Jim soon had a modeling contract with one of the largest agencies in New York. Within six months after stepping off a Greyhound bus, Jim's picture was appearing in all the high-fashion magazines. He'd be carrying a tennis racquet, with a white sweater loosely tied around his shoulders by its sleeves, smiling his million-dollar smile, becoming a well-known, highly paid male model.

The next step was an acting career. Encouraged to take lessons, he soon found himself in acting classes that had nothing to do with Stanislavski or The Actor's Studio. He was enrolled, on the advice of his modeling agency, in a TV techniques crash course, one of those training sessions designed to teach good-looking men and women how to speak a sentence with lots of facial expression and no regional accent. Six months after he began his lessons, he was headed for the Coast, signed by the largest talent agency in the country.

He got no work for six months. Then, one day, his agent called. There was a part in a new series for which he would be perfect. Jim was sent up, and after what he describes as an agonizing revolving-door audition schedule that stretched into weeks, he was informed that he would be one of the stars of the new show. His starting salary was nine hundred dollars an episode for thirteen weeks. If the show went beyond that, his contract would be renegotiated. Jim tells the story from there:

"Everyone was really friendly toward me—understanding, like they were almost sympathetic. I guess they knew I was scared to death playing a cop, wearing a uniform, having lines, doing a series. The money was good, but I'd made more as a model. However, after the first thirteen episodes were shot, we were picked up, and that's when it really became exciting. I was in a hit series. Just like that. I know it sounds like it never happens, but it happened. And that's when things changed. I was now making five thousand dollars a week, and the talk of money was one direction—up. The more ratings, the more popularity, the more I was willing to make personal appearances and build a strong identity with the public as my character, the more money was going to be in it for me.

"Acting, though, is a lot different from modeling, especially in terms of . . . stamina. You might do a job for a day, for two days, they might fly you to a location for a week, and you'll work twelve or thirteen hours a day, posing, but afterwards, you're off. I saw a little blow [cocaine] as a model, but I stayed away from it; I was afraid of it. I'd heard the stories, seen the disaster areas, the guys who missed calls, the girls who looked fucked-up at the age of twenty-five, their careers all but over. I wasn't a boy scout, but I wasn't, oh what can I say, risky. I was sensible I guess you could say. Maybe that's why I never got into it. You can't approach it sensibly, that's the whole point, isn't it?

"Well, things started to get a little rough on the set. I was in a very physical part, and week after week I'd be in car chase sequences, fights, 'arrests,' and lots of L.A. location work, which is very fatiguing. One day, as I came off the set, sweating like a bitch, ready to collapse onto a cot, this really good-looking guy came up to me, smiling, happy, confident. He said if we could go to my dressing room we could talk. If I weren't so dragged I would have said something like, who the fuck are you, but I just thought he looked like he belonged on the set or something. Anyway, we got to the dressing room, my dressing room, and this guy takes out a kit and starts laying a line [of cocaine] the size of a rattlesnake. I told him thanks but no thanks, and he put his arm around my neck, reassuring me, telling me I'd feel a whole lot better. And that it was the best type of cocaine. "What type is that?" I asked. 'Free,' he said, as he smiled.

"So I took the line, snorting half of it in each nostril. He was right. I felt great after that. I was ready to do my scenes, and at the end of the shoot, the director took me on the side and said I'd done some of my best work yet on the show. My friend was still there, smiling, his arms folded, occasionally talking to somebody, and escorting them to privacy.

"Everyone knows, everyone who uses coke knows that the more you take, the more you want. This was a classic case of induction, I see now, but I didn't know anything in those days. By the start of the following season I was spending, are you ready for this, first five hundred dollars a week, then a thousand dollars a week, then who knows how much. I was using blow all the time, on the set, off the set, in the morning, in the evening, all the time. My weight began to drop off. I'm a well-built guy, but can look wiry when I'm too thin. Even as a model I always had to keep weight on, especially for high fashion. You know, broad shoulders, muscular chest, strong legs, no waist. In those days I did weights a little bit. On the set though the work was physical enough, exhausting, and because of deadlines we sometimes shot seven days a week. When I wasn't on the set, I was learning lines for the next day, doing routines, practicing physical moves with our 'technical expert.'

"It was the tension in my face when I was away from my kit for more than a couple of minutes. I was gritting

my teeth a lot, swallowing, twisting my head on my neck.
Then the nightmares really began. I started missing re-
hearsals, then missing shoots. I was drained. I couldn't
sleep at night, I couldn't work during the day. I lost interest in the show, in my character, in my social life, in my
wife, in my home, in my looks, in everything except the
lines. Not the lines in the script, the lines on the mirror.
The show was still doing well, I was making over a half-
million dollars a year, with guaranteed income from eventual syndication, and, you won't believe this, I was broke.
Money to me meant tomorrow's blow. I couldn't get it fast
enough. The guy who had turned me on was always available. Sometimes the stuff was sent to my home at night by
limousine. The most beautiful women were his delivery
boys.

"Then, things got worse. The show began to slip in
the ratings. Instead of slowing the pace up and concen-
trating on each episode more carefully, the producers
pushed even harder, trying to get as many episodes completed before the axe fell. Don't forget each episode, even
if it never got to air, was still sellable in syndication, in
foreign markets. It was only a matter of time, though,
before the word came down from the network. We were
cancelled.

"I didn't care much at first. I was hot, I'd done the
teen magazine thing, and I'm sure the blow made me feel
even more invincible. But I didn't work. Not just right
away, but for a couple of years. The money went fast. I got
into tax trouble, I couldn't justify where it all went to, I
hadn't played it smart. I owed the government everything. I had to sell my house. I was humiliated to the point
where I was appearing, nameless and lineless, in TV commercials. Me—a teen idol, star of my own series—pushing
soda pop and deodorant. "I got an offer to make a movie
in Italy. A real low-life piece of shit. I did it because I
needed the money. Even then I was spending it on blow.
After the Italian movie, which was never released in

America, I got divorced. Then, finally, when the show went into syndication, some money came trickling back to me. Not a lot, certainly not like it had before, but enough to start me back on my feet. It was about this time I decided to kick. I stopped, cold turkey, and started working out, playing a lot of ball, getting sleep, hanging out at the beach. Eventually I got a shot at another series. It failed. Then another. It failed. Now, I'm in a new show, a kind of prime-time soap opera. It's something a little different. I hope it goes."

It didn't. Jim made four episodes of the show, which wasn't picked up by the networks. Today Jim lives modestly in a bungalow just outside of Hollywood and drives a used car. I asked why nobody threw the pusher off the set. Jim laughed and told me that the guy was on the payroll. He explained, that drugs keep everyone working harder; you know, the Peruvians-chewing-the-coca-leaves trip. Some can handle it, others can't. Those who can't are replaced by those who can. When things get out of hand, though, delays set in, and delays are the only real tragedies in TV. It doesn't matter if it's personality clashes or star temperament (which insiders will tell you is mostly drug disorientation), strikes, absenteeism, script rewriting, location problems—delays mean money. Everyone is paid on a time basis. Money adds to the overall budget, reflected in the licensing fees the networks pay for shows. Success spells money, money turns at least in part to larger salaries, larger salaries mean more drugs, more drugs mean more work, more work means more money. . . .

As I pointed out before, the networks don't pay out equal to the cost of producing a show, per episode, often forcing producers into the red. Realistically, however, a network isn't going to let a hit show fold for lack of cash flow—that would be ridiculous. A network will find a way to subsidize a production. It may opt to relicense immediately for late-night first syndication broadcast, or buy a future percentage of syndication profits. At this point, the network will add these new costs onto their overall advertising rates, which sponsors will then pass on to the consumer.

Incredible as it may seem, the TV-viewing, middle-American, middle-class public actually subsidizes life in Hollywood's fast lane when it buys a bottle of its favorite soda, or goes for the higher-priced spread, or decides which toilet tissue is really the softest. Sooner or later, part of the money will find its way into somebody's nose.

8 Items—1

1. Mr. Television.   August 1981. Milton Berle announced he was severing his last ties with NBC and making a new deal with cable. Milton Berle was the first of the "exclusive" stars to sign with a major network back in the early fifties. At the time, August 31, 1951, Berle signed an exclusive contract with NBC for thirty years. Since he was no youngster at the time, it was generally assumed that the contract was to last a lifetime. Berle outlasted the lifetime and set his first cable special, costarring Lucille Ball, Walter Matthau, Jack Lemmon, Tanya Tucker, and Dick Van Patten, for September. The irony of Berle's contract with NBC was that after his Tuesday Texaco Show faded from popularity, the network didn't know what to do with him. Toward the end of the fifties they humiliated the one-time king of top-line variety by making him the host of something called "Celebrity Bowling." Then he vanished from the network, which prohibited him from working anywhere else. His lifetime contract became a contract with obscurity.

2. Gary Coleman in pay fight with NBC. Gary Coleman, star of NBC's "Diff'rent Strokes," sought, on October 6, 1981, to renegotiate his contract with Tandem Productions, the independent outfit packaging the popular NBC sit-com. Coleman's starting salary for "Diff'rent Strokes" was $1,800 a week. His present salary is approximately $30,000 a week. His lawyers contend that even though his salary has increased, the fantastic success of the show is not properly reflected in Mr. Coleman's salary. Brandon Tartikoff, newly installed president of NBC Entertainment, conceded that "without [Gary Coleman] the show would not be commercially viable, and whatever shell of a show would be left would be unacceptable." Tandem, meanwhile, countersued its invaluable star for five million dollars in damages. The first episodes of the show excluded Coleman, who was biding his time at his Los Angeles home.

Gary Coleman is thirteen years old.

3. Johnny Carson bombs in England. A forty-minute version of "The Tonight Show," aired once a week in England, proved to be a national disaster. Signed by London Weekend Television, Ltd, Johnny was aired on Saturday evenings. The *London Standard:* "Who is this Johnny Carson guy? I find it very difficult to laugh when the chat-show king is earning a multimillion-dollar salary reading cue boards." The *Sun:* "To be frank, Carson got right up my nose." The *Daily Mail:* "His monologue could be in Swahili for all we get from it." Perhaps the best review, though, came from the *Sunday Times*'s Russell Davies: "The Tonight Show has catastrophically equated our national tastes with those of Benny Hill. [His guests included] a marmoset that peed endearingly on Johnny's head and an aardvark that shat in a sandbox." Carson, commenting in the December 21 issue of *Time* magazine, replied, "I never expected to be a tremendous hit in England." He wasn't. According to

Central Scotland Television: "Our audience didn't like it, and more important, didn't understand it. Seventy percent of the jokes mean Sweet Fanny Adams to us up here." And don't you forget it. "The Tonight Show" was dropped from London Weekend Television, Ltd, in the spring.

4. Sorry, Wrong Number. The ABC TV movie, "Pray TV," dealt with the burgeoning business of TV evangelism. No doubt pressure from the Moral Majority and the coalition accounted for the rather timid, ambivalent nature of the show. Nevertheless, the fictitious telephone number used in the film received more than 15,000 telephone calls from people wanting to make donations, after a plea was made for money from the fictitious preacher.

5. Coke Adds Life. Where do the great ideas for television shows come from? The previous season—1980–1981—a television commercial for Coca-Cola showed "Mean" Joe Green returning to the locker room, only to be stopped by a cute little tyke wanting his autograph. The kid offered "Mean" a sip of his Coke, and Joe burst into a smile.

On November 15, a sixty-minute NBC-TV dramatic special, based on the plot of that commercial, aired under the title "The Steeler and the Pittsburgh Kid." A Coke and a smile.

6. $uper Bowl. Speaking of football, here are some interesting facts about the Super Bowl. It is estimated that one hundred million Americans, approximately one out of every two men, women, and children, watched the game on Sunday, January 24, 1982. The previous Super Bowl attracted 47.2 percent of all viewers in homes with televisions, just six percentage points below the "Who Shot J.R." episode of "Dallas," the most-watched TV episode in television history. The advertising cost of thirty seconds on the 1982 Super Bowl was $345,000, with twenty-three available minutes. They were all sold out as early as the first week in December. CBS, handling the broadcast, used one hundred microphones, twenty-three cameras, four Chyron graphics generators (responsible for the statistical information that flashes on the home screen), fourteen videotape machines with slow-motion capability and instant replay, and a Telestrator, for hand-drawn diagrams over a still shot.

Here is a breakdown of the cost of a thirty-second spot in the last ten Super Bowls:

1973	$ 90,000
1974	100,000
1975	110,000
1976	125,000
1977	125,000
1978	185,000*
1979	180,000
1980	234,000
1981	275,000*
1982	345,000

*These games started at 6:00 EST. All other games were played in the afternoon.

The players in the National Football League are threatening a strike for the 1982–83 season, for greater pay and retirement benefits.† The average professional lifespan of a football player is under four years, the shortest in professional sports. Sunday's heroes are generally

†The players went on strike September 24, 1982.

acknowledged to be the worst-paid of all professional athletes. One final note: late in the 1982 season CBS announced that it expected to charge one million dollars a minute for the 1984 Superbowl.

7. Videotaping receives unexpected interference. The federal appeals court on October 19, 1981, decided that the seven million owners of home video recorders were lawbreakers every time they taped a show off the air. The ninth U.S. Circuit Court of Appeals said that the manufacturers, distributors, and retailers were liable for damages because they were aware that the recorders "would be used for such purpose and induced, caused or materially contributed to the infringing conduct."

All of this is the result of an ongoing lawsuit brought about jointly by Universal City Studios and Walt Disney Productions against the Sony corporation, four retailers, an advertising agency, and one private citizen. The case was appealed to the Supreme court.

8. University of Southern California to create a film–TV school. In 1981, George Lucas, Irvin Kershner, and Randal Kleiser, all graduates of USC, jointly contributed huge sums of money toward the construction and operation of a film–TV program at USC. Along with his contribution, George Lucas had this to say: "Film and visual entertainment are a pervasively important part of our culture, an extremely significant influence on the way our society operates. People in the film industry don't want to accept the responsibility that they had a hand in the way the world is loused up. But, for better or worse, the influence of the church, which used to be all-powerful, has been usurped by film. Films and television tell us the way we conduct our lives, what is right and wrong. It's important that the people who make films have ethics classes, philosophy classes, history classes. Otherwise we're witch doctors. . . . Film-school graduates end up making commercials for their local TV station or medical films to train doctors at their local medical school. The opening ceremonies of the 1984 Olympics will be seen [on television] by two and a half billion people. It's only prudent that the people who are managing that information have a rich college education."

Any part of the film–TV complex not built by 1984 will have to wait until after the Olympics, because no construction will be allowed on the campus while it is in use as an Olympic Village to house the athletes. In spite of Lucas's $4.7 million donation, the necessary $14 million figure had not, as of June, 1982 been realized. Oh yes, Steven Spielberg donated only $500,000 to the complex. But then, he was turned down by USC and was forced to attend a state college.

9. Cubism. The season premiere of "NBC Magazine" featured a story about the phenomenon of Rubik's cube. The story was built around the premise that the cube was neither bad nor good, just popular. "NBC Magazine" was canceled at the end of the season. The reason: the show wasn't bad and it wasn't good. It just wasn't popular.

10. Good Sport. On September 12, 1981, not even Jerry Falwell could prevent what went out over the airwaves. Vitas Gerulaitis, annoyed over a bad call by a linesman, threw a temper tantrum that the CBS director decided to cover in close-up with a shotgun mike. Therefore, the entire country heard Gerulaitis scream, "One goddamn foot over the fucking line!"

Of course, why this type of language is excusable in real life (if a tennis court constitutes real life) but is absolutely forbidden in dramatic presentations that are supposed to heighten the drama of life remains a mystery— apparently even to the Moral Majors.

11. CBS announces it will produce forty movies for theatrical presentation. CBS Theatrical Films was formed early in 1982 for the purpose of producing movies. This wasn't the first time a network tried to get into the big-screen business. It wasn't even the first time CBS tried it. Twelve years earlier, both CBS and ABC had active movie divisions, and both lost bundles of money. Last year, CBS decided to try again, producing the unsuccessful Sally Fields vehicle, *Back Roads*.

That TV studios should want to make movies is fairly predictable. First, as movies become more and more expensive to make, their licensing fees have skyrocketed, making the margin for profit that much slimmer for the networks. Also, increased competition from cable TV for the rights to films has produced a more competitive seller's market. Therefore, it seems logical that the networks would try to develop and control their own feature films, for eventual broadcasting (or cable leasing) at a larger profit. There is a lingering danger in all of this, and that is the risk the networks run of unfair competition charges from the Federal Trade Commission. In the late forties, the government ruled that the major movie studios could control only two of the three branches of their business. At the time, the studios made the movies, handled their distribution, and owned the theaters in which they played. "Monopoly," cried the government. The settlement provided for two out of three branches of the movie business to be retained by the studios.* This was the beginning of the rise of the independent producers, who eventually found their way to television.

While the major studios had tried to control product, distribution and exhibition, unfair competition was charged because there were *only* seven major film studios. In television there are at present only three major

---

*Production and distribution were most often retained by the studios.

commercial broadcasting networks (a fourth, Dumont, was forced out of business in the early fifties because of a lack of available affiliates). One reason the networks have shied away from more extensive in-house production is the ever-present fear of governmental regulation stemming from the charge of monopolistic activities involving production, distribution and exhibition. It was big news, then, when CBS announced it was going back into the movie business. However, if the government didn't overreact, it may have been because CBS quickly announced that Michael Cimino, director of the forty-million-dollar disaster *Heaven's Gate*, was going to direct the first feature.

9 The Ratings—2

The ratings for the final presweeps week were as follows:

TOP FIFTEEN SHOWS	NETWORK	RATING
1. "World Series Game Six"	ABC	37.2
2. "60 Minutes"	CBS	30.5
3. *Every Which Way but Loose*	CBS	29.2
4. "M*A*S*H"	CBS	26.4
5. "Dallas"	CBS	24.9
6. "Three's Company" (tied with) World Series Pregame Show, Game Six	ABC	23.9
8. "NFL Postgame"	CBS	23.8
9. "Too Close for Comfort"	ABC	22.6
10. "NFL Monday Night Football"	ABC	22.2
11. "Hart to Hart"	ABC	21.9*
12. "Laverne and Shirley"	ABC	21.9*
13. "Little House on the Prairie"	NBC	21.9*
14. "CBS NFL Football Game"	CBS	21.9*
15. "Love Boat"	ABC	21.4

Network Averages: ABC: 20.4   CBS: 19.7   NBC: 15.6

---

*The reason why shows 11, 12, 13, and 14 aren't tied has to do with share differentials.

On to November, the first sweep month, the first month that "counts." Presumably, the audience has had the opportunity to look at the new shows and review the old ones. With the holiday season about to break, increased revenues from advertisers gearing up for the Christmas push allow for more expensive programming from the networks, as well as increased competition.

Ratings books are based on three key months, demographically analyzed as the most significant of the year. They are November, February, and May. It is on the basis of these sweeps months that shows make it or break it. Predictably, the networks offer their best, hoping to win and win big. Future rate-cards for advertising will be based on sweeps performances.

The three networks geared up for the first test of the 1981 season. CBS announced that for Thanksgiving it would run the Clint Eastwood smash-hit movie, *Every Which Way but Loose*, which made over fifty million dollars in domestic rentals. ABC promptly countered with an announcement that it would be showing *The Goodbye Girl*, Neil Simon's hit movie, a forty-million-plus hit. NBC decided to go with its controversial "Death of a Centerfold: The Dorothy Stratten Story," hoping that a first-run, never-before-seen, controversial made-for-TV feature would beat out the competition. In other scheduling maneuvers, CBS planned to devote an entire evening to an airing of *Mary Poppins*. NBC slated a Bob Hope special saluting the sixtieth anniversary of the National Football League, followed by a Frank Sinatra special, and ABC scheduled *Moonraker*, a James Bond film. The total cost to the networks for these shows, just two evenings of competitive programming, was in excess of twenty million dollars.

ABC also scheduled "special editions" of two of its hit series, "The Greatest American Hero" and its newest hit, "The Fall Guy," for the first sweeps week. NBC countered with the potential blockbuster TV-movie, "For Ladies Only," about male strippers, with very interesting costar Patti Davis, daughter of President Reagan. CBS threw in a highly edited version of *10* (approximately a 5), while ABC had *Grease* for week two. It was going to be quite a month to stay home and watch television—a fact not lost on the movie studios, which gear their Christmas feature release schedule to coincide with the end of the sweeps. December, March, and June are traditionally the lowest rated months of the TV year and the highest for movie theater attendance.

Going into the November sweeps, the networks still hadn't completed the beginning of the new season. "Dynasty" and "Benson" hadn't begun airing new episodes, and shows such as "Open All Night" and "Darkroom" had their premieres delayed by the network decision to build up the openings as "events" for sweeps.

Sports continued to play an important part of the network battle for viewers. Football, building to its traditional winter climax, was holding forth in the top fifteen for its prime-time ABC Monday-night broadcast. However, the baseball play-offs, traditionally a ratings winner and a high ticket item, were way off base. The lack of viewer interest was blamed on the strike-caused split season. The first eight games of the play-offs scored a full 25 percent less of an audience than a comparable viewing period the year before. The ratings of play-offs, divided between two networks (NBC carrying the National League, ABC the American), were identical, reflecting what had been true since the fifty-two-day baseball strike had taken place: the public simply wasn't willing to play ball with the big leagues after being laid off during the summer. ABC was understandably jittery about how the World Series would fare as its lead into the sweeps—there would be as many promotions for November shows as there would be commercials for tires and razor blades.

The World Series, though, grew in interest and drama as the Yankees swept the first two games before losing Graig Nettles, and the Dodgers, revitalized and reenergized, took the Series back to Los Angeles for a dazzling four-game sweep to the top. It was a key Series, in more ways than one. The network that wins the bidding wars for the World Series, in this case ABC, hopes more than anything else that the Yankees play the Dodgers because the games are then played in the two biggest television markets. When other teams are in the World Series, the numbers are inevitably down. Los Angeles versus New York is a dream Series for television. As the games played off, the ratings grew. Game six, the final game of the World Series, drew an unbelievable 79 percent share in Los Angeles and a 62 percent share in New York—gigantic numbers.

Fortunately for NBC, the series ended in six games. Game seven, if it had been played, would have gone opposite the debut of the fall lineup on NBC, Thursday night (game six, the clincher, was delayed one day because of a Tuesday rainout, finally played the following night, Wednesday, which would have put the seventh game into an unexpected Thursday slot). Someone at NBC, sweating out the final innings of a Dodger Series-ending victory, commented that "if the series goes to seven, we're hopeful that the Afghans will invade the Bronx and the President will call off the game." NBC was on a phenomenally unlucky streak. Millions had been lost by the network when President Carter announced that the United States wouldn't be participating in the Olympics in 1980, the year NBC had bid twenty million dollars for the rights to carry, as one executive put it, "the games that never were." The Emmy broadcast for 1980 was boycotted. The Super Bowl, another NBC coup for 1981, was all but preempted by the return of the hostages. The attempted assassination of President Reagan in 1981 occurred on the same day NBC was slated to cover the NCAA college basketball national play-off game. Even the "Hill Street Blues" sweep of the 1981 Emmies was bittersweet; because of the writers' strike there were no new episodes of the show to be broadcast until October 29. If a seventh World Series game had been played, it would have gone up against the police show's season opener. As it happened, ABC, in broadcasting the rain-delayed Tuesday game on Wednesday, had to preempt its own seasonal premieres of one new series, "The Fall Guy," and one returning hit, "The Greatest American Hero." As they say, that's the way the ball bounces.

The first week of the November sweeps showed a sharp race developing for the season leadership. ABC finished ahead of the pack with a 19.2 overall rating, with CBS coming in a strong 18.4. The surprise of the first week was NBC's strong showing in spite of their lack of blockbuster programming to lead into the sweeps. Regular series fare saved the third network. Interestingly, "Love, Sidney," the controversial sit-com, showed a strong fourteenth, in spite of The Coalition for Better Television.
New series rumored to be in danger of cancellation by the end of the first sweeps week were "Mr. Merlin," "Gimme a Break," "Jessica Novak," "Nashville Palace," "Code Red," "Maggie," "Lewis and Clark," and "Fitz and Bones."
Here are the complete Nielsen ratings for the week ending Sunday, November 8, 1981:

PROGRAM	NETWORK	RATING
1. "Dallas"	CBS	27.4
2. *Grease*	ABC	25.1
3. "60 Minutes"	CBS	24.8
4. "Dukes of Hazzard"	CBS	24.1
5. "Three's Company"	ABC	23.1
6. "Facts of Life"	NBC	22.2

PROGRAM	NETWORK	RATING
7. "Love Boat"	ABC	22.1
"Magnum, P.I."	CBS	22.1
9. "M*A*S*H"	CBS	22.0
10. "Monday Night Football": Minnesota-Denver	ABC	21.9
11. "Too Close for Comfort"	ABC	21.6
"Archie Bunker's Place"	CBS	21.6
13. "Born to Be Sold"	NBC	20.9
14. "Benson" (season premiere)	ABC	20.7
"Love, Sidney"	NBC	20.7
16. "One Day at a Time"	NBC	20.3
17. "Real People"	NBC	20.0
18. "Fantasy Island"	ABC	19.8
19. "Happy Days"	ABC	19.7
20. "Mork and Mindy"	ABC	19.4
21. "Laverne and Shirley"	ABC	19.3
22. "House Calls"	CBS	19.2
23. "Hart to Hart"	ABC	19.1
24. "Barbara Mandrell"	NBC	19.0
25. "Private Benjamin"	CBS	18.9
26. "Championship Boxing"	ABC	18.6
27. "Little House on the Prairie"	NBC	18.5
28. "Hill Street Blues"	NBC	18.4
"The Jeffersons"	CBS	18.4
30. "Father Murphy" (premiere)	NBC	18.3
31. "Best of the West"	ABC	18.2
32. "The Fall Guy"	ABC	18.1
"The Greatest American Hero"	ABC	18.1
"Taxi"	ABC	18.1
35. "Barney Miller"	ABC	17.8
"The Dukes of Hazzard" (Tuesday)	CBS	17.8
"Alice"	CBS	17.8
38. "That's Incredible"	ABC	17.7

PROGRAM	NETWORK	RATING
39. "Quincy"	NBC	17.5
40. "Ripley's Believe It or Not"	ABC	17.2
"CHiPs"	NBC	17.2
42. "Walt Disney"	CBS	17.1
43. "Today's FBI"	ABC	17.0
44. "The Gauntlet"	NBC	16.9
45. "The Incredible Hulk"	CBS	16.5
"Trapper John, M.D."	CBS	16.5
47. "20/20"	CBS	16.5
48. "Lou Grant"	CBS	16.2
49. *Revenge of the Panther*	CBS	16.1
"Other Victim"	CBS	16.1
51. *The Two of Us*	CBS	15.8
52. "Flamingo Road"	NBC	15.7
53. "Mr. Merlin"	CBS	15.6
54. "The Princess and the Cabbie"	CBS	15.3
55. "Diff'rent Strokes"	NBC	14.5
56. "WKRP in Cincinnati"	CBS	14.1
57. "Gimme a Break"	NBC	13.9
58. "Jessica Novak" (premiere)	CBS	13.4
59. "Nashville Palace"	NBC	12.8
60. "Making a Living"	ABC	12.6
61. "Harper Valley"	NBC	12.5
62. "Code Red"	ABC	12.4
63. "NBC Magazine"	NBC	12.3
64. "Here's Boomer"	NBC	11.3
65. "Maggie"	ABC	11.2
66. "Legacy of Maggie Walsh"	NBC	11.0
67. "Lewis and Clark"	NBC	10.4
68. "Fitz and Bones"	NBC	6.8

The second and third weeks of sweeps month went to CBS, with an overall 19.4 rating, as opposed to ABC's 18.6 and NBC's 15.4. CBS won with its regular programming against a host of special "events" on ABC. CBS continued to dominate Sunday nights, leading strongly with "Archie Bunker's Place," and "Dallas" dominated Friday; CBS managed to dominate four nights to ABC's three and NBC's none. The much-edited *10* managed to score high in the ratings. Over at NBC, "Father Murphy," which had started off strong, dropped to forty-seventh place. "Flamingo Road" also slipped down in the ratings. A "special," "The First American Ultraquiz—Part One" was a total washout for the network. The best news for NBC was minimal: "Real People" had shown its highest numbers to date during sweeps.

Strong November showings went to "Magnum, P.I." and "Knots Landing," both CBS; "Barney Miller" on ABC; and "Hill Street Blues" on NBC, coming in 19.1 with a strong 34 share.

With sweeps month drawing to a close, it was clear that CBS was continuing its long-term domination. NBC, however, was floundering, and badly. Predictably, the new leadership blamed the old, claiming that the "honeymoon" still wasn't over.

It is an unofficial rule in television that the network doing the poorest will stay with its new shows the longest. On the other hand, the hottest network will drop new losers as quickly as possible. The first show to be cancelled in the 1981–1982 season was ABC's "Maggie," followed in quick succession by "Jessica Novak" and "Shannon," both on CBS.

10 The Independent Producer: An Interview with Garry Marshall

Garry Marshall arrived in Hollywood in the fall of 1962 to write for the "Joey Bishop Show." This newest of careers for the boy from the Bronx joined the list of leader of a jazz combo, reporter for the *Daily News,* and joke writer for comics Phil Foster and Jack Paar. Years later, when their respective fortunes were somewhat reversed, Marshall hired Foster to play a supporting role in "Laverne and Shirley."

While working in television, Marshall met and teamed up with Jerry Belson to form one of the most successful comedy-writing teams television ever produced. They wrote over one hundred sit-com episodes for such classic series as "The Danny Thomas Show," "The Lucy Show," and "The Dick Van Dyke Show." They also wrote dramatic episodes for "I Spy" and "Chrysler Presents." In addition to their extensive television work, the team also wrote for movies, doing the scripts for *How Sweet It Is* and *The Grasshopper.* Eventually, Belson and

Marshall split the team up, each turning his individual attention more fully to feature films.

It was with "The Odd Couple" that Garry Marshall first tried his hand at producing as well as writing for television. The success of the show's five-year run thrust Marshall to the top of the coming age of independent producers.

ELIOT: *Let's begin with the Moral Majority.*

MARSHALL: Well, there was a whole flurry about the Moral Majority, and everybody was asking everybody about it. It's really not my most passionate subject because I don't seem to be involved with what they seem to be battling about. My particular type of show has always been in the eight o'clock family hour. At that hour the audience is a mix of adults and children. The Moral Majority was attacking mostly sex and violence. I heard my shows were on lists. In checking this out I found it not to be true. I found there was a list they had made indicating they were going to monitor my shows, and others, just to see what the results were going to be. On that list was "Happy Days," and an incident of one particular episode of "Laverne and Shirley" that had a controversial mail poll, not from the Moral Majority, but just from certain parts of the country. In that particular case, I agreed with the mail, it wasn't the right episode. We did an episode that dealt a little too comically with drugs in a couple of spots.

Most of my shows have been on for a number of years and have always had the same profile. When I heard that "Happy Days" was being investigated, and all this, my answer then was that if you checked the country and took a survey, my feeling would be that "Happy Days" was much more moral than Jerry Falwell. So I don't think it's even anything to discuss with my shows. As far as theory goes, I am not a believer in the theory that a certain pressure group should dictate what's on television. I think the freedom to do shows is what has made television, and what has made our country. I don't think anyone can dictate what goes where, as far as the free airwaves goes. Television has its own censorship.

ELIOT: *How does television censor itself?*

MARSHALL: The networks have their own censors, advisors, consultants, and the people who make the shows themselves. I have three children: I have no interest in putting things on television that I can't sit and watch with my children. I never felt censorship was much of a problem. However, when pressure groups do come in I don't think it's particularly right. The reason I don't think the Moral Majority is the worst thing that ever happened to the country is because I think something, in a sense, good came out of it. In the very greedy, competitive atmosphere that television entered into in the late seventies, the censorship, the taste, the class, the dignity that television had prior to those years went downhill. The greed, the competition caused the networks to put on material that I myself felt was not proper. Specifically, as much as I would defend, and say the Moral Majority has no right to come in and say you should do this and that on your shows, on the other hand if they would help stop putting on television shows like when that little girl was raped with a broomstick, then I am totally for the Moral Majority.

I think some people in this country just felt television was going berserk, and rightly so, the guys running it were just throwing on anything and somebody had to speak up. I think they did speak up. However, to speak up under a religious banner of a certain group leading them, I don't know if that's the proper thing. I think the Moral

Majority might have helped television regain its senses. Taste is not subjective; class is. So I am somewhere in the middle. No broomsticks, and no censorship by pressure groups.

I did a rather sensitive show on "Happy Days," examining the fact that blindness is a rather frightening experience and has to be dealt with. On this particular episode, Fonzie is temporarily blinded, and doesn't know if he's going to be able to see again. It was a sensitive subject and a sensitive show, if not so much about blindness than about overcoming all adversities, and how to deal with it. That was what the show was about. In the competitive atmosphere of that year, the network advertised that show with pictures that said, "Fonzie can't eye the girls anymore" and there was a promotion where he was standing with two hot girls, a promotion which had nothing to do with the episode we wrote and produced. In their attempt to get titillation through a sexual hype, that's the way they advertised it. That caused me to quit, and to announce that I was closing the entire show up. I got apologies from the network, saying it was a mistake, it would never happen again, and it was because the other network was putting on topless . . . and that was the whole atmosphere. That was about two years ago, just before the Moral Majority began its big push. I think if you're looking at it sociologically, when the ABC network, which was traditionally third, started to rise and became number one, it shook up the whole industry and everybody in it got crazy. I think it's calmed down now a little bit, and people have come back to their senses.

ELIOT: *Do you get a lot of pressure from the network when you try to do a "Happy Days" show that has a point behind the humor, like the Fonzie blindness script? Wouldn't the network rather have straight comedy?*

MARSHALL: They don't love them. The ratings don't change, the networks just feel that they might change, they might go down. When we do "the sensitive shows" the networks get nervous. Or anything cultural, they get nervous. We did a show about ballet, with a prima ballerina, exposing seventy-five million people to ballet, and they got extremely nervous, they weren't sure when to run it, they weren't sure what time of the year was best . . . it still was number one in the ratings. They just feel it's risky, and why risk when you're dealing with all this money?

ELIOT: *Is the Fonzie promotion you described really that awful? After all, not being able to ogle pretty women would be one of the worst aspects of being blind for a guy like Fonzie. In fact, I think the advertisement is a quite perceptive one.*

MARSHALL: But it hyped it to where it was an insult to the people making the show. Not only that, but I know something about marketing. The show simply wasn't about Fonzie worrying about not seeing pretty girls, it was about his not seeing. The worst thing you can do to an audience is fool them. If they tune in looking to see "hot," and they see a "sensitive show," they're going to get angry. So I think it's even a bad marketing ploy.

ELIOT: *What about the strikes? I would assume you were on the side of the producers?*

MARSHALL: I was on both sides. My personal approach, I don't kid myself, I'm a producer, an executive-producer, I'm a director, I'm a creative whatever, but basically everything I've accomplished or attained has all come true because I was basically a writer. I was good enough so that in order for them to "get" me they had to give me these other things. So I still have my first allegiance to the Writers Guild. Even though I'm management now in a sense, I have to be on both sides. I was a picket, a captain of a picket line, in fact. I'm in every union there is so I'm also in the actor's union. I didn't picket for them, but I did help raise money for them.

ELIOT: *How do you think the strikes affected the 1981–1982 season on the air?*

MARSHALL: It affected my season probably a little differently than it affected other producers. I work in a unique way. I build families in order to do shows because I'm trying for long runs. In order to do that you build units, you build teams. I built some very good teams: actors, writers, crews, etc. By the time of the strike, each unit had been working at least three years together. When the strike hit, the studios, or management, whatever you want to call them, to make up some of the money lost on the strike started cutting salaries and personnel in the shows. Many of my "crack teams," as I call them, were broken up. I lost crew members, I lost key personnel because of cutbacks to make up for the strike. A lot of my guys went to Canada to work because of the length of the strike. So in a sense it was very uprooting for my whole organization. It hurt and I still haven't replaced the people. In some cases we took up collections to help out guys who got hurt bad. Not big-deal organized things, just within the shows themselves—it was a mess. Morale-wise, it was a killer. Business-wise it put us behind schedule, we had to rush, and the episode quality, etc., I don't think was up to par. A lot of the new pilots were totally wrecked. I'm not doing that many new things, but guys coming up, with new ideas, new concepts, and new shows probably got hurt badly.

ELIOT: *Maybe, in fact, the strike helped those shows already established, by the very fact of hurting the* *new shows, shows which would eventually be competing for the established timeslots.*

MARSHALL: Well, the shows that had been running could rig up and go faster than the new shows, once things were settled. We did have a little advantage in that sense. The reverse of what you say is what the business end of the networks say, about quality, about preparation time, etc. "It doesn't matter. The audience didn't notice."

ELIOT: *Perhaps the quality may be overlooked by the public, but what about the fact that on page one of the local newspaper the faces of men and women making thousands of dollars a week are shown on strike, while the fellow buying the paper is bringing home a hundred and fifty dollars?*

MARSHALL: Outside the TV community, I don't think there is support for any of the strikes. And I don't see why there should be. Except, of course, there are a lot of people who work in the industry who don't "take home thousands." And they did get hurt, badly, by the strikes. The strikes affected everybody in Hollywood; this is an industry town. It affected actors, writers, directors, agents, crews, cameramen, restaurants, everyone. But for people working in the coal mines of Pennsylvania, I don't think they should have any sympathy whatsoever. Television is not the most important thing in the world, and for those it is it shouldn't be. My shows deal with friendship, family, etc. Most of the country is lonely. Television is a great, great friend. For those people to lose certain friends it is sad, but on the other hand there were no blank screens. It's been proven time and again that the avid television watcher prefers reruns anyway. They like the reruns; they don't bother them. And they're happy.

ELIOT: *How do you account for the remarkable success of your type of television: "Happy Days," "La-*

verne and Shirley," "Mork and Mindy," "The Odd Couple"?

MARSHALL: The three shows, "Happy Days," "Laverne and Shirley," and "Mork and Mindy" are big, but were bigger a few years ago.* I had "The Odd Couple" on for five years. It was successful, but never achieved the same popularity as the three that I have on now. It is an inexact science; it has a magic to it, television. It's like saying, here you are, a hundred different friends to choose from and which friends do you want? You choose the ones you think will be better for you. There's no way to figure it out; nobody ever has. I don't have a formula or anything else. I do have a philosophy, though. I've always felt that some of what you may call your corny or sentimental emotions still are very strong in this country; friendship and family are two of them. In New York and L.A. they like to laugh. The rest of the country likes to laugh too, but they read more into the shows. When "Happy Days" was so big, it gave a lot of people the opportunity to think back to the period of the fifties. It gave them peace, it made them less nervous. A lot of sociologists have written about "Happy Days." "It calms people down," I remember one sociologist writing.

I always thought it was broken down into thirds, why a show is successful. One third is the creative concept. Is it a good cast, is it a concept that is right for people? Then there's one third that is timeslot. Where it is placed in the schedule. Many good shows fail because they're not placed at the right time in the schedule. The third third, some call it luck, I call it "time in history." Like all entertainment and all phenomena, there is a time in history. Whether it's clothing, fads, food, books, television, mov-

---

*"Mork and Mindy" was cancelled at the end of the 1981–1982 season.

ies, it's all the same. Time in history is an important factor in a show's success. "Happy Days" came at a perfect time in history. Had "Happy Days" opened in the sixties it would have died. It opened right at the seventies, when people wanted something nice, don't give me a headache, I had it already.

"Laverne and Shirley" opened at a perfect time in history, one of the few shows that debuted number one in the ratings. First night on, number one. Perfect time in history, because after being pressed by literature and movies saying that women have rights, all these women depicted were always middle- or upper-class. Laverne and Shirley are the first lower-class women ever shown to a mass audience. The reaction was immediate. "Finally us!" "Lucy," which we've been compared to, was similar, but not lower-class. We were closest to "Lucy" in comic style. I worked for Lucy for three years, and she taught me everything which I taught my sister [Penny Marshall] and Cindy [Cindy Williams]. Lucy, remember, always represented housewife, not blue-collar. So, again, time in history for "Laverne and Shirley" was perfect.

Fred Silverman was important also. When "Happy Days" was on, and a hit, he needed another show, badly. He was pushing me very hard. He was pushing for another spinoff of "Happy Days," this time starring Fonzie. He felt that Fonzie as a blue-collar mechanic would work just like William Bendix worked in "The Life of Riley." I didn't want to push Fonzie out of "Happy Days" because I felt he was half the premise of the show, contrasted against Richie. The bargaining came from Silverman, who said, give me another show and I'll put it in a good timeslot. I kept on saying, I don't want to do another show, I'm happy with "Happy Days." "You gotta do another show, we need it," Silverman kept insisting. I said, okay, but let's make the blue-collar workers women, and not men. He gave "Laverne and Shirley" the half-hour following "Happy Days," which is a pretty good timeslot.

"Mork and Mindy" didn't have a good time slot. It started out badly because of that. Now, most people feel there is a cold, calculating business side of television which is separate from the creative side. In fact, it's more often the case that the creative side is what, in turn, brings the business side into being. My resisting pulling Fonzie out of "Happy Days" was a creative decision which led to "Laverne and Shirley." "Mork and Mindy" was even more of a case of a creative decision leading to a business one, instead of the other way around. It began when the network came up with the brilliant notion that, now that we had created the timeslot, eight to nine o'clock Tuesday nights, they were now going to break up the shows, and expand the viewing audience, figuring that the people would find the shows, and new ones would fill the familiar timeslots. At the time "Happy Days" and "Laverne and Shirley" were one and two in the top five shows. The network figured it was a natural way to bust open another night.

In sit-com strategies, the hardest timeslot to fill is the eight o'clock half hour. It's the anchor for the rest of the night. Not only is it hard to do, most of your best creative people, especially the writers, don't want to do them. I'm one of the few that wanted to write the eight o'clock shows. My peers, who came up with me in the business, all chose to do nine-thirty shows because you can be more sophisticated. I had five wonderful years with "The Odd Couple" at nine-thirty and was very happy with that.

ELIOT: *Why is "The Odd Couple" a nine-thirty show and "Happy Days" an eight o'clock show?*

MARSHALL: Demographically, "The Odd Couple" doesn't have the appeal to the younger audience. At eight o'clock you have to get the kids and you have to get the adults too. "Odd Couple" didn't have that strong an appeal to kids.

ELIOT: *Back to "Mork and Mindy," though, and the timeslot strategies.*

MARSHALL: Right. I told the network when they said they were going to break up "Laverne and Shirley" and "Happy Days," "You're going to kill me." Again, not for business reasons, but because I had created this wonderful flow, they went naturally from one show into the other. It boiled down to the fact that the network told me, flat out, they were dying on Thursday nights. I said, instead of busting up my shows, give me a crack at making a new show, if you'll leave my other shows alone. With "Mork and Mindy," the show had no time in history whatsoever. People were nodding off watching television. The premise of the show was totally irrelevant. I was looking for a unique performer who would just blow everybody out. By accident, really, we found Robin Williams. He was a last-minute replacement on the pilot episode for "Mork and Mindy," which was an episode on "Happy Days," and he just burst out. When the network saw the show, though, they weren't that impressed, and then they started talking about Mondays. Then I did the first "Mork and Mindy" show, which ran an hour as a special. The network took one look and said, "You've got Thursday!" It opened on Thursday, it opened big, went to number one the first year, made the whole Thursday night, they had everything, and then they started moving the shows around anyway. Politically, yes, you fight for timeslots, but I think it's mostly from the creators to protect themselves, to protect their product.

ELIOT: *What about your failures? Whom do you blame, your own creative judgments, or the network business people?*

MARSHALL: I once made a "bad" show that wasn't a bad show. It was a mistake. ABC blew it. The network, traditionally, has not been able to break Saturday night at eight o'clock. I created a show for that timeslot. It was the perfect Saturday night at eight o'clock show. It was called "Blansky's Beauties." It went on the air, it beat "Mary Tyler Moore," not by much, but it held the highest rating ABC ever got in that timeslot in fifteen years. It ran for a half year. There was a little internal trouble with it, it was a hard show to make. It was expensive, I didn't have enough time for it personally, I was busy and I don't like to do too many shows at once. . . . They cancelled it. Since then, they haven't had a show that's worked in that time-slot.

Last year, during the strike, I had nothing to do, I figured I'd give them one more attempt at capturing Saturday night, eight o'clock. I came up with a show they looked at, they didn't like, and they didn't put on. I still think they're wrong.

ELIOT: *What prevents you from taking that show to another network, NBC for example?*

MARSHALL: Not loyalty. Just contracts, star commitments. If a star is in a show, and it doesn't go, you just can't take that star to another network. I suppose, though, if I really wanted to, I could get whomever I wanted at any network. I'm not like a lot of other producers, I'm not interested in having a million shows on the air. I do them on whim more than anything else. Aaron Spelling pushed to have nine shows on the air, that's what they're in business for. Norman Lear wanted to have a million shows on at the same time. I've never had the desire. Just by sheer luck and faith I got more than one show on at the same time. I'm happy doing one show at a time. I'm not interested in being a corporate head. That's why I float. I do a play, I do a movie. Every once in a while I get an idea

I'd like to try, or the network looks like it's about to ruin one of my shows and I say, Jesus, I better give them this . . . something else so they'll get off my back.

ELIOT: *What about the influence of cable on network television?*

MARSHALL: Cable is interesting to me, since I'm not looking for that corporate structure. I'm like a traveling guy with a bag. "Hey, what's in this town here?" It interests me. It's an opportunity to try shows that may only have limited appeal. I've always been in the business of making shows that have mass appeal. Some of the ideas I get do not have mass appeal. I feel cable might be the outlet for those ideas. For example, a show about geriatrics. Nobody would touch the subject at the networks. Maybe I can find a place for it on cable. From what I understand, you don't need seventy-five million people watching you on cable to be a hit.

ELIOT: *It's remarkable that the networks wouldn't think geriatrics a good, captive audience.*

A MARSHALL: I agree with you, I think it is a mass market yet to be tapped, but the networks don't think so. Sometimes the business is a little crazy. Look, the studios are making shows for the networks, and they're also making movies for the competition, cable, and pay-TV. Regular TV is saying it's okay, pay-TV is saying it's fine. It's like that wonderful line from Shaw: "When you rob Peter to pay Paul, you rarely get a complaint from Paul."

ELIOT: *One final question. Which really came first,* American Grafitti *or "Happy Days"?*

MARSHALL: "Happy Days." They took the pilot I made for "Happy Days," which was part of the "Love, American-Style" series, looked at it, cast Ronny Howard because he was the star. The network didn't buy the series, they said nobody cares. Then the movie [*American Grafitti*] was released, and *Grease* was also a smash on Broadway. The network came back and said, let's put it on. It bothered me a while. George Lucas was mad at me because he felt I cut the movie. I did beat him into the little towns with the show. But we're all friends now.

ELIOT: *Thank you.*

11 The Network Executive

Without doubt, the most well known network executive in the history of television is Fred Silverman. His reputation is enormous, matched perhaps only by his penchant for keeping his name in the papers and in the minds of TV viewers. Because he has done time at all three networks, Fred Silverman's contributions to modern commercial television must be acknowledged as singularly influential, perhaps more so than any other network executive. While the legends of General Sarnoff of NBC and William Paley at CBS are long standing, their influence on programming policies, particularly in the area of entertainment, is at best minor; Sarnoff gained his reputation in the days of live TV drama, while Paley is known more for his views on news coverage than for entertainment.

Fred Silverman rose rapidly through the network ranks during the sixties, his finger on the pulse of television-watching America. By the time he arrived at NBC in 1978, where he'd been brought in to turn things around, he'd already worked his magic at CBS and ABC. At CBS, Silverman picked up the pieces of the shattered Jim Aubrey era of the early sixties, when the network suffered its worst overall decline. After leaving CBS, Silverman was able to turn ABC from a joke into the top-rated network. Even the ABC news department benefited from his talents. ABC news, at best the kid-brother tabloid to the prestigious CBS and NBC news divisions, made enormous strides under Silverman.

The reason ABC News jumped from third place in the ratings to a consistent first or close second has often been attributed to the expansion of the duties and responsibilities of Roone Arledge, from head of ABC Sports to head of ABC Sports and ABC News, an appointment made by Fred Silverman. Silverman realized that what was missing from the ABC network news broadcasts wasn't the news; all three networks had that. Nor was it reporters in the field; they were expendable, interchangeable. What was missing was the concept of entertainment imposed on the business of news. The "serious" news attitude, dominant in television since the days of Edward R. Murrow, was, well, old news. How to contemporize the news without making it frivolous? The solution was pure Silverman.

Barbara Walters's contract with NBC News was coming up for renewal. There are regulations within the television industry regarding "tampering" with network news reporters, not unlike the contracts major league teams abide by with respect to their players. TV News divisions pride themselves on being "above" the entertainment world. News anchors, and in ever-increasing proportion the field reporters, regard themselves as journalists. Years earlier, this was demonstrated quite clearly when AFTRA (the American Federation of Television and Radio Artists) went on strike, pulling all entertainers off the air. Newscaster Chet Huntley, then the coanchor of the NBC Evening News, returned his AFTRA card and continued to appear on the air, maintaining that he wasn't in the business of variety, he was in the business of news.

There is, however, a brief period when it is possible for a rival network to "raid" the competition. This occurs during contract renewal time. Often, through indirect channels, feelers will be put out to determine what it will take to get a newsperson to "jump." The Barbara Walters episode took place at just such a time. Silverman's offer to Walters was irresistible: if she would leave NBC for ABC, Silverman would make her the first woman news anchor at the network level in the history of television. Walters had come closer than any other woman to this cherished, prestigious appointment.

Naturally, there was a catch. Part of the deal was that Walters would coanchor the ABC Network News with Harry Reasoner. It was something neither side liked. However, Reasoner was under contract, and, for a million dollars a year, Barbara Walters could try.

Eyebrows were raised everywhere when the coanchor plan was revealed, including up at ABC headquarters along TV Row in New York City. That, of course, is the difference between a Fred Silverman and the hordes that would be king. What no one could see at the time was the clear picture of Silverman's vision. The "mismatch" of the century copped headlines across the country. The considered opinion was that Walters and Reasoner would be the disaster of the year, the decade, the century!

Rumors of arguments between the two anchors even before the first broadcast came flying out of ABC with noticeable regularity and an unusually detailed recounting of events; it was almost as if ABC *wanted* the feuding to be public. America was told, day by day, that Harry Reasoner just didn't like Barbara Walters and was chagrined at having to share the venerable, male anchor-seat with a woman. Walters, on the other hand, bit her famous lips and held her head up, refusing to fight in public.

The popular sentiment was decidedly with Reasoner. Walters, her personality more ape-able than affable, came off as pushy, gaining corporate advantage just because she was a woman. The highly publicized one million dollars a year didn't help either.

The one indisputable result of the appointment of Barbara Walters, though, was the sudden jump in ratings. This, of course, was what Silverman had in mind all the time. People everywhere tuned in to see the explosion (on camera, they hoped), pushing ABC News out of obscurity and into a new income bracket.

The loser resigned gracefully. Harry Reasoner threw in his chips when his own contract came up for renewal. He returned to CBS, to resume his place as coanchor of "Sixty Minutes," a show he had helped to launch ten years earlier. While the ratings at ABC News naturally declined as the tumult faded, they never receded back to where they had once been. Even when Barbara Walters was removed from nightly duty, there was an element of satisfaction involved. The "bad guy" of the episode was dethroned. When Walter Cronkite finally retired in 1981, ABC News was more than ready to compete regularly for the number-one position in the news.

Cut to 1981. NBC. "The Tomorrow Show." The ratings are sagging. Fred Silverman is the determined head of the third network, brought in to do for NBC what he'd done for CBS and ABC—to save the day.

Close-up of Fred Silverman, alone in his office, pondering what to do, looking for the right move.

Dissolve to Rona Barrett, gossip reporter for a great metropolitan network, ABC. She is dishing out the dirt on "Good Morning America," ABC's answer to NBC's "The Today Show," consistently outranking NBC and CBS in the morning network ratings. However, as popular as Rona Barrett has become, she is not happy with her handle as gossip mavin and has stated many times she wants to be regarded by the public as a legitimate journalist.

Close-up of sweat on Silverman's brow. Flops like "Supertrain," the series that never left the station, have tarnished his mantle of invincibility. He needs to come up with something, and fast. A headline event, something to bring attention to the network. Aah, he thinks, putting his feet up on his corporate desk. Duplicate the ABC strategy: the immovable object vs. the irresistable force.

It was simple. He would lure Rona Barrett away from ABC with the promise of making her a legitimate newsperson, a *journalist,* bumping her from early mornings to late nights as the costar of a new, expanded version of "The Tomorrow Show." It was a beautiful plan. Carson had been publicly slapping Silverman's wrists for months, both in the opening monologue and in the front pages of the more hysterical tabloids. Carson had been threatening to take a walk if "The Tonight Show" wasn't shortened to one hour. Finally, Silverman gave in, Johnny got his way, and the ratings took a nose dive, as more and more viewers started to check out ABC's "Nightline," with the unlikeliest of Carson-killers, Ted Koppell. Now, Silverman could put it to Carson with a revamped ninety-minute "Tomorrow Show," complete with a split studio setup connected to Burbank—Johnny's own turf—at Rona's Hollywood hacienda.

Of course, there was one hitch. Rona Barrett would be the new cohost of "The Tomorrow Show." If Harry Reasoner had been cranky when forced to share his seat with Barbara Walters, Tom Snyder went absolutely wild.

Sure enough, the headlines crackled from front pages across the country, and America stayed up late to see the most interesting nighttime war since Jack Paar attacked Ed Sullivan's "exclusive" guest star policy back in 1961.*

---

*Sullivan was furious that guest stars he'd paid thousands for appearing on his late night show were popping up on "The Tonight Show" for $320, often on the Thursday or Friday before they were scheduled to appear with him. Sullivan finally announced that any guest appearing on "The Tonight Show" would be banned from "The Ed Sullivan Show." Paar, in a fury, broke into his own Friday night "Best of Paar" rerun to publicly blast Sullivan. The feud erupted into

The ratings for "The Tomorrow Show" were never higher. Silverman could envision the controversy lasting for months. He promised the network that by December 1981 NBC would be number one in the ratings.

Rona Barrett, though, wasn't about to hang in limbo while Tom continued to thumb his nose at her in public. Incident after incident culminated in a furious behind-the-scenes battle for control of the show. The very first broadcast between Tom and Rona resulted in the new costar nearly walking off the show. Tom had a large, Jerry Lewis-style projection screen on the set, so that he could see Rona live from Burbank. Rona, though, only had an earphone, so she could hear but not see. The reason, according to NBC, was cost—twenty thousand dollars for the extra two-way video line. Barrett's people felt it was calculated to make her look bad. Insiders felt it was done on purpose, to exacerbate the bad blood between the two. Rona came off like a blind person in a crowd, while Tom guffawed at her in public. It was an auspicious start.

A short time later, Barrett walked off the show in midtaping, disgusted with Snyder's lack of cooperation. She claimed that her contract called for a specific amount of time during the first half hour of the show and that Snyder was hogging it all, pushing her further and further into the tail of the ninety minutes, regardless of her commentary, regardless of her guest stars. She came back to the show for a while and was given the "celebrity reports" spot on the network "The Today Show." That was all well and good, except that she had had that at the more popular "Good Morning America," without the late night aggravation.

---

a war, never fully resolved, even though Sullivan eventually agreed to "bury the hatchet" to "prove" there was no bitterness between the two men. There are those in the industry who still chuckle at Paar's hijinks, insisting that it was all a well-thought-out publicity stunt, boosting the ratings of both shows.

In October, Barrett announced that she was off "The Tomorrow Show" forever. The network promptly announced that she would be starring in her own weekly prime-time show, "Television: Inside and Out." The costume-drama title was only a foreshadow of this extremely boring, ill-planned, poorly received exercise in frustration. Even with the mythic Mick Jagger as her premiere guest, "Television: Inside and Out" was sixty-sixth in the ratings and went down from there, bottoming out at seventy-third—of eighty prime-time shows. Cohosting with Rona was the aging Pat Weaver, creator of the original "Today Show," looking far less formidable than Tom Snyder (and far less threatening), and Gary Deeb, the Chicago TV critic who seemingly hates television: not a great choice for a show about the medium, broadcast on a Saturday night. "Television: Inside and Out" was all washed up after five shows. Rona left the network and was rumored to be in Europe, letting off steam. Silverman was left behind to pick up the pieces.

It might all have been academic. By June 1, while Barrett was still in the thick of her feud with Snyder, and "Hill Street Blues" was still tracking down a regular time slot, Edgar Griffiths, chairman of RCA, parent company of NBC, resigned. By July 1, Thornton Bradshaw had taken over as chairman, announcing that Brandon Tartikoff would be promoted to the head of programming. When the newly appointed Tartikoff was asked by a reporter from *The New York Times*, if he lacked the authority to make certain decisions, he reportedly replied, "Can I get back to you on that?"

12 Independent Production

The following round-table discussion was took place in a small bar in Venice, California. "Laura" is a combination of several staff members and network executives who wish to remain nameless, for obvious reasons. "Fred" is a pseudonym. All the dialogue is verbatim. The topic of discussion was the production of a new NBC series, St. Elsewhere, slated for airing in the fall of 1982.

LAURA: I work for a company that supplies the networks with product. When you work for a network, you're at their mercy. They dictate at a lot of levels what you do. It's real interesting when your show has the kiss of death to it. It's like having the plague or something. All of a sudden network people aren't answering your phone calls. What keeps a show on the air is the advertising, the numbers. When the show goes to pieces it's something like the fall of Saigon.

Everyone who works in production has total disdain for the people in the networks, because they think if they knew what they were doing they wouldn't be working for the networks. Which is totally true.

Last March, we get this call from NBC at MTM, they want to do another show like "Hill Street Blues": "We want something we can put on the fall schedule this year." Brandon Tartikoff made the call. Two staff writers were then assigned to write the pilot. The first thing you do is make a presentation film to show to the affiliates, to get this thing rolling. Then the strike sets in. It doesn't end until August. Now it's August. The script is submitted, and nothing happens. Also, during this time, what happens is Grant Tinker taking over NBC, replacing Fred Silverman, who's responsible for the original concept of "Hill Street Blues." Now, we suddenly become the first MTM show on NBC in Grant Tinker's regime. Ironically, it was Silverman who kept "Hill Street Blues" on the air.

So now it's September and we're waiting. What's going on? Then the process begins. You deal with people in development. There's this meeting. Brandon Tartikoff says to us in this meeting how much he likes this script. He wants to give us a script order so we have lots of lead time. The name of the show is "St. Elsewhere." It's a hospital set in Boston where the people working there would rather be anywhere else than there. He says what NBC wants to do is make a pilot for the fall (1982). Then we want some time for refinements, so we can put in on the schedule the following September, of next year. Far out. We're kind of pleased.

Now we've actually got a script order. Only, the script order never actually arrives. They're having trouble negotiating the pilot. It was obvious, to do it right, it was going to be a very expensive pilot to do.

ELIOT: *How expensive was it?*

LAURA: One-point-seven million dollars. For a one-hour pilot. That was the amount we wanted from the network. Whatever overage there was going to be would be in addition to that. It had to look right; it was going to be an inner-city hospital. We were going to have to build a terrific set—there wasn't a hospital available for us to just go into and use. Plus it had to be equipped for intensive care, more than just a bedpan. A lot of things were going to be happening at the same time. It was going to be a very expensive pilot. The network wanted to give us one-point-five million, we were holding firm for one-point-seven. Two hundred thousand dollars was separating us at this point. Now we're into the beginning of October, and now there's a problem.

They want to make a show but they don't want to commit to the money to make the show the way it should be made. At the same time, the script order, remember, still hasn't come over. All that time could have been spent preparing scripts. However, without the order, you just can't proceed to that stage. What it really came down to was that no one was really able to make up his mind what he wanted. There were two prevailing theories on our side as to why.

The first was simply that NBC didn't have the money. They had a miserable year, the disaster with the Olympics, everything. So maybe they don't want to make any pilots this year. Okay, in that case, how about committing to six shows, so we can amortize the cost of the expensive set, down the line? Meanwhile, we're getting kind of itchy. Many of us have been nominated for Emmies in the past couple of years, and there are opportunities coming at us every day. We don't like being jerked around.

The second theory was pretty interesting. We began to wonder if there wasn't a reverse nepotism going on, a variation on a paranoid theme, if you will. Maybe the feeling at the network was, oh no, not another Grant Tinker project. It's strange, because Grant Tinker is no longer actively associated with MTM. However, the public knows Grant Tinker as Mary Tyler Moore's ex, and that together they formed and were successful with the company. As far as they're concerned, Grant Tinker is MTM.

Another unusual aspect of "St. Elsewhere" is that usually you're trying to sell an idea to the network. You pitch it, you song and dance it, whatever it takes. But this was their idea. Fred Silverman wanted another inner-city show. It was the same with "Hill Street Blues." In that respect the guy had vision.

ELIOT: *To what extent would you attribute the delays to a case of nerves, a situation of fear at the network to risk putting on another "hip" program on the order of "Hill Street," with the Moral Majority looking over their shoulder? I understand "Hill Street" is not a favorite of the conservative right?*

LAURA: One of the major problems you have doing commercial television is "Programs and Practices" at the network you're dealing with. There are a lot of things they won't touch, and a lot of things they do trade-offs on.

One of the set stories is about a doctor who contracts VD. The story centers around who he gave it to at the hospital, tracking it down. It was handled in a responsible way. Nevertheless, the network decided not to do a show about VD. Cancer: fine. Even though these were doctors, VD was off limits. Especially this year. "Here's our suggestion," they said. "Use herpes instead."

ELIOT: *What's the difference?*

LAURA: Herpes is incurable. Get it? The moral overlay compensates for itself. In other words, the story of herpes is the *tragedy* of herpes. The easy logical road is, "Extramarital, or premarital, or sex in any form other than to procreate is a no-no."

Anyway, they reassured us that in spite of the fact we couldn't come to terms on the story, on the budget, they still wanted to give us a script order.

ELIOT: *What exactly is a script order?*

LAURA: The next step, although it still isn't yet the pilot stage. All it really means is that we now have a basis to negotiate the pilot. If they like the scripts. March 1980, though, isn't October 1979. There's a lot of time that gets eaten up before a pilot is shot, a lot of time. Scripts have to be written, adjusted, rewritten, and then, most important, they have to be cast. All of this can take months, and the network is talking about debuting this series fall 1981!

The reason why the core is so important to a successful show is that, the nature of television being so episodic, you're never finished with a project until the series has come to a final end. You're literally at the studio or in the office seven days a week. You have no life of your own. The core group keeps the show looking the same, sounding the same, and in a certain flow that hopefully keeps it in prime-time. Actors come and go, even stars sometimes leave a show. Writers do one, maybe two episodes of a series a season; rarely are they involved in more than that. It's the staff that runs a show creatively. The other side of it is that a good staff that believes in what it's doing will feel that a show not properly handled is being, in effect, taken away from them by the networks. You will become attached to a show in more ways than you realize. It's all-consuming. There's a reason for—what's the phrase this year?—burnout, for people getting into burnout so much. That's what good work will do to you. That's why the drugs are everywhere. They gunk the engine, so to speak, to prevent premature burnout before the network has gotten its pound.

ELIOT: *Do you think "Hill Street Blues" will make it?*

LAURA: The numbers have been incredible. Of course, they've gotten a twenty-one-gun send-off, and all the attention in the press. It's the hippest show in television.

ELIOT: *I'm not so sure of that. The first couple of episodes, it seemed as if the network were going out of its way to make sure no one could find it.*

LAURA: Yes . . . yes. . . .

ELIOT: *"Hill Street" was on a different night every week, or so it seemed. The thing about the show that was so striking then was the way each hour didn't come to a neat end . . . that the shows stopped rather than ended, and were loosely tied together in a real blues motif. This season, the early episodes seem so much more academic. There are neat little endings, and overly cute passages. The characters, in an incredibly short time, have become parodies of themselves. The lawyer, the public defender, the captain, the captain's girlfriend, the eccentric plainclothes detective, they all comment endlessly about . . . themselves. The delicate balance they had seems to me lost in a distorted awareness. It's as if they all woke up and said, "Hey, we have a hit on our hands. Let's keep doing what we've been doing." I thought the whole point was the innovation, and the promise of so much more.*

LAURA: As a matter of fact, the network did think the stories were too diffuse last year. It's going to be interesting to see what happens with "Hill Street." There have been script changes, extensive script changes this year. The big difference is, in a sense what you've pointed out, that of all the loose ends they used to have. The network wants one of those loose ends tied neatly by the end of the hour. In other words, the show has to have one beginning, one middle, and one end; the rest okay, can dangle.

ELIOT: *But that's a big, big difference . . .*

LAURA: Oh yeah.

ELIOT: *And would give me something to think about if I were about to "recreate" "Hill Street Blues" in a hospital.*

LAURA: Right. If they want something else, they ought to say so.

ELIOT: *Any stars to attract the audience?*

LAURA: No. It's going to be ensemble, like "Hill Street Blues." It's interesting, though, that NBC wouldn't mind having a star in "St. Elsewhere." For that, they're ready to spring. Their feeling is rather old-fashioned, that a star is a strong drawing card. One look at the history of the last couple of seasons will quickly show how wrong that is.

We finally had this climactic meeting. It was long, grueling, and, we felt, for the most part, successful. Until we looked around the room and saw there was no one there from NBC with the power to make a decision. The most important member of the NBC programming department was the Head of Dramatic Development. It's simply a de facto of life that episodic television is a producer's medium. Not because producers are so visionary, or so influential, it has nothing to do with that. It has to do with the fact that nobody on the network side knows how to make decisions.

ELIOT: *Where would you put writers on the authority scale?*

LAURA: Low. Staff writers have more importance than free-lancers, obviously, because they're going to be involved with more than one or two episodes. The main function of a staff writer is to "fix the script."

ELIOT: *That sounds like you expect poor scripts to be delivered.*

LAURA: It's never a question of a poor script versus a little undisovered gem. Free-lancers don't know a show the way the staff does. The staff will take a script that may be terrific, and shape it a little more here, a little more there, so that it becomes, in a sense, interchangeable in the rotation of play-offs. "Fixing" doesn't imply that a script is good or bad. Just that it has to conform to a certain body of work. As it happened, most of the "St. Elsewhere" scripts were done in-house. With the strikes, and the constant delays, and the fact that this was a new show, the chances are that if you do manage to hire free-lance writers, fifty percent of the time the script will come in bad. As a staff writer, you wind up fixing other people's fuckups. It's a high burnout risk, and there's a little avarice involved, granted, but the bottom line is the show has got to work.

FRED: I was a director of development for NBC up until June of this year. My job was to work with the vice-president in charge of development at the network in buying shows for the network. People come in and pitch ideas for shows. The ones we like are then put into development by the network, working with an independent production house most of the time. From the scripts we buy, a certain number of pilots are made. From those pilots, the shows for the following year are bought. I was involved with a show called "Flamingo Road," and the development of "Fame." I first got the idea to turn *Fame* into a TV series when I went and saw the movie.

ELIOT: *There seems to be a new trend developing, turning movies into shows. "Private Benjamin," for example. However, with "Private Benjamin," there was a fundamental flaw in the transition. Most of the humor and intelligence of the original script was built around the idea of a nice Jewish girl suddenly finding herself in the Army. For reasons unfathomable to me, the girl—Private*

Benjamin—on TV is not Jewish. The entire concept has changed. Why bother to buy a film if you're going to discard everything but the name?

FRED: For the name. The assumption is that a successful movie will have a huge carry-over audience. With *Fame*, I saw immediately that we had the opportunity, at NBC, to do something new, something fresh, and also to crack a timeslot we've never been very successful in: the eight to nine o'clock hour, the "family entertainment" time. There was some resistance. Shows about show business don't do very well. On the other hand, shows about high school do. "Bracken's World," for example, lasted only a couple of weeks; that was a series about life on a Hollywood set. "Room 222," "White Shadow," and so many others. "Our Miss Brooks," there's another one. So NBC bought the show if the emphasis were to be put on the students who happen to be at this special school, but who have the same problems that kids in school say in the Midwest might have. The key point of relating is kids with dreams. All kids have dreams. These kids dream of fame.

I saw the movie and the next day went to Brandon Tartikoff, president of the network, and told him we should buy the movie immediately and develop a pilot. Silverman, still at the network, agreed, and we bought the rights to the show as a television series. The commitment to get the pilot written cost, loosely, in the forty-thousand-dollar range. However, once you make that commitment, you're also committing another million and a quarter, conservatively, to shoot that pilot. In the old days it was easier, because you made, in effect, two one-hour pilots and played them on the air sooner or later as a movie of the week, more or less insuring a return on your investment. The problem with that was, simply, the pilots didn't look like the weekly shows. It's called a "premise pilot"—how the characters got to where they are, who they are, why they are, etc. This is a big difference from how the characters are going to be, week after week. Also, for a premise pilot, you have to load up on stars, to insure a movie-for-TV play-off. These stars are usually not in the series. So the trend today is to one-hour pilots with a set cast.

So that's what we did. We made a one-hour pilot. There was a change in concept from the movie in that we added a new character, a kid a little more hayseedy, from the Midwest, so that more kids could relate easier. We tried to keep as much of the film's cast as possible. We even went so far as to use the same music from the movie, to make it easier for the audience to accept the concept as a weekly series.

The pilot was received well at NBC, but the show wasn't put on the fall schedule. There wasn't a place for it. NBC has not had a lot of success with situation comedies for the past couple of years. ABC, on the other hand, dominates in that field. If you want to introduce a new show, part of the strategy is in the timeslot. If there's a new sit-com that ABC wants to break, they can slot it behind "Three's Company," and you can bet a lot of people are going to see what the new show looks like. With "Fame," there wasn't any place to put the show on the schedule. So it was held back for the January "second season," when the first crop of shows has gone through a sweeps period, and those that didn't do well have been canceled. Even so, Fred Silverman had enough faith in the show to give us a go-ahead to order six episodes. What happened is, as a result of the strike, there was almost no time to let new shows develop. As soon as the first numbers came in, the January replacements were notified to gear up and start production. Normally, a pilot would then be shot; this year there is no time for pilots, so NBC lucked out with a show ready to go. Today, any pilot being shot is in preparation for the fall 1982 schedule.

Part of the network's job is to be able to understand the potential for a show. This comes under the heading of "franchising." It's what happens when a "genre" show hits; then all the shows for the following season have a similar look. That's the cyclical effect, or "franchising" of an idea. The show that remains the exception to all of this is "Lou Grant." Nobody in the industry understands how this show stays on the air. There is no such thing as third-person drama on television.

ELIOT: *Third-person drama?*

FRED: With a "Magnum, P.I." or a "Hill Street Blues," the main characters are an integral part of the action. They are involved, first-person, with the plot. Journalists are third-person heroes; they watch the action, they follow up on the action, but they're never the action. At best they're background. This is the reason there haven't been a number of journalism shows following in "Lou Grant's" footsteps.

[Author's note: "Jessica Novak," the adventures of a female reporter for a local television station, was one of the first shows canceled during the 1981–1982 season.]

ELIOT: *Aren't you confusing action with drama? And isn't all drama on television repetitious? The hero always wins; the bad guys always get caught; stars are never killed off. I would guess there are those who would say "Lou Grant" is a very dramatic show, if not necessarily an action show.*

FRED: Action serves as drama on television. The word "drama" can clear out an executive meeting faster than a bomb scare.

From the *New York Post*, June 1, 1982:

Trouble on the set of NBC's new project series "St. Elsewhere"—a hospital show modeled after

"Hill Street Blues"—has cost producers an estimated $1 million.

MTM Enterprises, producers of the show slated for Tuesday nights beginning next fall, threw out more than six days of shooting after becoming dissatisfied with the pilot episode.

The director and one lead actor, Joseph Summers, were replaced.

Shooting resumed in California three weeks ago "with everything back on track," said an NBC spokesman.

The spokesman declined to confirm that the loss was $1 million but admitted "it was a lot."

13 The News

It all really began more than thirty years ago, when television was still a flicker in someone's sty. While puppets on strings and clowns with seltzer bottles dominated the screen, there were a few pioneers who felt that television, like the early film industry, would eventually outgrow short pants and aim for a more mature crowd. By the time Edward R. Murrow became television's first adult authority figure, with his exotic, stone-cut facial features so essentially correct for the early gray-and-white TV screen image, television news had begun to grown up.

But if the screen has brightened considerably since the frigid days of the cold war, the memory of those times has certainly dimmed. While it's common knowledge that CBS heroically took a strong stand against McCarthyism, with Edward R. Murrow and Fred Friendly seeming like two idealistic horsemen tilting at the windmill of supression, CBS also employed one of the most vicious, lengthy blacklists in the fifties, a list that some claim still exists today.

The point is, finally, not whether CBS was the good

guy or the bad guy, but that CBS was able to take a stand at all. It's one thing to follow a tradition; it's another to begin one. The only other news reporter with a regularly scheduled network in those early days was John Cameron Swayze, the authoritative news announcer with fifteen minutes of no-nonsense headlining on rival NBC. It was still the era of single-sponsorship, with Swayze's name and image linked forever with the Reynolds Tobacco Company, a relationship unthinkable in today's era of fractionalized sponsorship and the doctrine of separation of program content from commercial product.

With the exception of Edward R. Murrow (whose image was so popular that he was gradually removed from hard news after the fall of McCarthy to wind up hosting the rather innocuous "Person-to-Person"), very little progress was made in television news reporting. It wasn't until the newspaper strike of 1962 in New York City that things began to change.

New York City was then still the base of most live programming on the networks, and all news programming. The city was also the center of print journalism, with a half dozen of the country's most prestigious newspapers still in operation. The newspaper strike lasted several months and eventually resulted in the demise of the *New York Mirror,* the *New York Herald Tribune,* the *New York World-Telegram and Sun,* and the *New York Journal-American.* There was an information gap in the country's largest city, for its general population and also for the networks, which depended more than casually on the combined services the newspapers provided for them. Television's electronic journalism borrowed heavily from print, with TV news bureaus staffed marginally and overseas bureaus virtually nonexistent before the days of satellite reporting.

The local "O and O" ("owned and operated") TV stations in New York City—WCBS, WNBC, and WABC—collectively seized the moment to justify expanded news coverage on the local level—coverage that would by necessity provide substantial national and international reporting, since the network news broadcast was still fifteen minutes in length, including commercials. By the time the strike ended, the nightly local newscast was an accepted fact of life. Such early luminaries as Gabe Pressman suddenly found a new world to conquer: the world of respectable local TV journalism.

Right after the expanded local broadcast came the expanded network news program, from fifteen minutes to a half hour. It was the beginning of the era of Walter Cronkite and Huntley-Brinkley.

The next step in the growth of TV news occurred one day in November 1963, when a bullet ripped its way through the brain of the President of the United States as he rode, smiling in his limousine. The events in Dallas thrust TV journalism into the forefront of mass communications. What was unique about the coverage of the Kennedy assassination was the number of live cameras on the scene. In 1963, the era of hand-held, porta-pak equipment, coupled with electronic editing, videotape replays, and image storage was still years away. This meant that news, for the most part, was reported after the fact, with hours between event and presentation, because of relatively slow film processing. The Kennedy trip was occurring in the aftermath of the Adlai Stevenson visit to Dallas, a visit that saw the distinguished statesman spat upon by residents of the Texas city. The media overload covering what was essentially the first campaign of the 1964 presidential race was decidedly excessive. There were dozens of newspeople from all corners of the country on hand. The equipment was already in place, so that in the aftermath of a modern American tragedy, everybody could share in the ritual of mourning. The TV journalists were notified well in advance when Lee Harvey Oswald was to be transferred from one location to another, affording the first broadcast of an actual murder, a moment in

TV history never likely to be duplicated. Those four days saw the maturing of a cumbersome, also-ran branch of American journalism, electronic news reporting, from a catch-as-catch-can operation to the head of the journalistic class.

The very presentation of the famous four days was also a revolution in kinetic reportage. Never before had TV cameras been so outdoors: live, presenting the unrehearsed, delivering the emotion of the crowd as well as the motion. The flow of material gave the events in Dallas and Washington a strange elegance. Until then, television news was thought to be encapsulating rather than the expansive reflection that Dallas proved it could be.

From 1963 through the late seventies, the undisputed leader in the reporting of news on television was CBS. The wartime, trenchcoat instincts of Edward R. Murrow were refined by the familiar, distinguished presence of Walter Cronkite. NBC, the best "second-day" news network, which made up in analysis what it lacked in immediacy, was slow in capturing those elements so vital to the drama of newscasting. At ABC it would take the grittiness of Roone Arledge to bring the network out of the journalistic stone age. By the middle of the 1981–1982 season, ABC was regularly outranking NBC and challenging CBS for possession of first place in the standings.

The 1981–1982 season saw many changes and transitions in the presentation of network news gathering and reporting. Perhaps the most significant event was the introduction, in July 1980, of Cable News Network, the twenty-four-hour all-news station commandeered by Ted Turner from his base of operations in Atlanta. By 1981, CNN was fully established, providing the first round-the-clock coverage of events as they happened. Turner succeeded in breaking the Washington–New York perspective on news reporting, the rush to "get it all in" in the approximately twenty-two minutes the nightly network broadcast allowed. The service was offered without cost to cable viewers; Turner figured, correctly, that most cable operations would gladly pay the approximately fifteen cents per month per household subscription fee to be able to offer an all-news channel. This gave Turner a potential audience of better than six million homes, and gave his audience the latest in technological satellite efficiency, along with a slightly southern point of view.

If Turner's all-news network was a success, it was strictly a succès d'estime, as it lost millions of dollars annually. By the end of 1982, rumors of CNN's pending demise or sale were being heard daily. Meanwhile, WPIX in New York was using satellite technology to assemble a news network of its own, the Independent News Network, linking more than seventy local, independent stations to a nonnetwork national and international news broadcast. The estimated audience was fifty million households. The flagship station, wholly owned by the Chicago-based Tribune Company, was reportedly doing extremely well, with a projection of more than three hundred affiliates hooked up to the independent news operation within two years.

Further, as soon as CNN proved that it could attract a sizable audience, CBS, NBC, and ABC announced plans to affiliate their news divisions with cable operations. By June 1981, ABC-Westinghouse was on the air with a rival, all-news, all-cable station.

Why is the nightly network news important to a network? Every executive will tell you the same thing: the ratings are secondary to the integrity of reporting the happenings of the day (every executive except those who work for the top-rated news telecast). While journalistic ideals may play a role, that's not the whole story. In fact, the network news plays a key role in the viewing habits of millions of Americans. It's well known in the industry that the station with the highest rating for the news will almost invariably carry a greater audience into prime time than the competition. Several years ago, the network prime-time block of programming began at 7:30. The FCC, in its never-ending quest to wedge the government into the affairs of private broadcasting, ever on the lookout for what it considers unfair broadcast practices, deemed that the half hour following the news belonged to the affiliates. What this meant was that the carry-over audience from the network news broadcast had an additional half hour before going into prime-time viewing (6:30 central time; the half-hour slot between 7:30 and 8:00 is supposed to be used for "community-related" programming, which means is that the time belongs to the affiliates, most of whom have filled it with game shows— "strips," as they're called in the industry—which traditionally make a large profit). The networks were vigorously opposed to this plan, claiming that the community-programming concept was a total flop.

In March 1981, Walter Cronkite, the dean of network news anchors, reached CBS's mandatory retirement age of sixty-five. His retirement meant many things to many people. William S. Paley, eighty-year-old chairman of the board, lavished praise upon Cronkite. His face made the cover of virtually every publication in America. To the rival networks, his retirement signaled a renewed competition for dominance of the evening news viewing audience.

The first major victory in the network news wars went to Dan Rather. CBS assured the hard-hitting reporter that he and he alone would fill Cronkite's position. Rather happened to be in Dallas on that day in 1963, and his on-the-spot reporting of the terrifying events are credited with establishing the then-unknown reporter as the new kid in town. Rising dutifully through the ranks, including a ratings-boosting stint as one of the hosts of the venerable "60 Minutes," Rather enjoyed his greatest popularity during the Watergate scandal, his no-nonsense style a constant relief from Nixon's lip-sweating sloppiness. Rather even exhibited some real old-style "Americanism" when, as he reported, he had to chase two shadowy figures from his living room late one night with an old-fashioned shotgun during the height of Watergate.

If Rather was the victor in the battle for Cronkite's job, Roger Mudd, another popular network reporter, was certainly the victim. Abruptly, upon hearing the news that Rather was the one, Mudd resigned from CBS. He was infuriated. After all, Mudd felt, he had done the hardest time the past dozen or so years, not Rather. Mudd had taken the heat for "The Pentagon Report," which blew the lid off frivolous defense spending, back in the days before Watergate. Mudd had gotten Ted Kennedy to agree to an interview in the fall of 1980, an interview credited with helping to destroy Kennedy's campaign for the nomination as the Democratic Party's choice to run against Ronald Reagan. Surely, Mudd felt, he deserved better than this. NBC assured him he would get it on their side of the street. As the ink was still drying on Roger Mudd's new NBC contract, John Chancellor announced that he was retiring as the sole anchor of the NBC Nightly News. The network promptly announced that Chancellor would become the new "commentator" of the network news report. While the assignment as commentator is certainly a prestigious one, on TV Row it was generally acknowledged as a step down made to look like a step up.

Then, on July 2, 1981, reportedly after extreme backroom pressure put on Roger Mudd, William J. Small (president of NBC News) informed the press that Mudd was not going to exercise his contract's option to be sole anchor of the News, evidently part of the package that had brought him to NBC. Shortly after that, Small announced that John Chancellor would be replaced by the anchor team of Roger Mudd and Tom Brokaw. Brokaw, host of "The Today Show" for several years (having replaced John Chancellor when Chancellor stepped up to the Network News), had reportedly applied his own pressure to Small. Brokaw's contract was about to expire with NBC News, and there was talk that ABC was trying to lure him to fill the still-vacant New York desk of the "ABC World News Tonight" evening broadcast.

"World News Tonight," meanwhile, was making plenty of noise with its innovative triumvirate of anchors: Max Robinson reporting from Chicago, Frank Reynolds at the Washington desk, and Peter Jennings, via satellite, from England. ABC was the only news report with a fully staffed overseas anchor, headed by Jennings, who shared anchor duties with his partners from across the Atlantic Ocean, going on the air at midnight, London time, five nights a week. Still, ABC had no one at a New York desk. This was seen two ways, depending on who was watching. To eastern viewers, it was an unusual style of reporting. To the rest of the country, it made for perhaps a more balanced, perhaps more accurate point of view toward reporting the events of the day.

ABC was not without its problems. Early in 1981, Max Robinson made an angry speech to a Chicago convention deploring the shortage of blacks engaged in reporting for the network news. Robinson, a black, infuriated the ABC executives. There was talk that he would be dismissed summarily, a move that reportedly caused further in-fighting at ABC. Some people thought the firing of one of the few blacks in network news might cause more trouble than needed, particularly when so few percentage points separated the three newscasts.

Back at NBC, Brokaw's salary as coanchor was reported to be the same as Mudd's: approximately one million dollars a year for approximately eight minutes of air-time, five nights a week. NBC announced the new anchor team with great fanfare. A much quieter announcement from the network had to do with NBC's abandoning, for the moment, expansion into the cable news area. The thinking at RCA was that the investment would go farther within the mainstream of network programming. The aim was for a nightly news program aimed at a previously untapped audience—the insomniac trade. The target was 2:00 AM news programming. CBS abruptly announced that it, too, was looking at late-night and early-morning newscasting. However, CBS was quick to point out that NBC was looking at a one-hour broadcast, while CBS was intent on a four-hour marathon that would bring the station directly into its morning network news.

One person seemed to be overlooked in these frenetic negotiations. David Brinkley was at that time the commentator of the "NBC Nightly News," having assumed the post when Chancellor became sole anchor. On September 10, 1981, David Brinkley announced to the press that he was retiring after thirty-eight years with NBC. "I'm leaving because there's nothing at NBC that I really want to do," Brinkley said. Insiders reported that Brinkley was angry at being bounced off the network news broadcast to make room for Chancellor's commentary. Some at NBC felt Brinkley thought he had had the first call to the anchor seat. Loyalty was never a big factor in big business, but thirty-eight years must have meant something. Everyone agreed that there was no way NBC would let Brinkley leave.

"I'm in good health, and it has nothing to do with money," Brinkley insisted. His weekly news magazine, NBC's attempt to produce a "Sixty Minutes," was cited as one of the reasons Brinkley was not given the nod to anchor. The show was always at the bottom of the ratings. Of course, the fact that it was slotted against the top-rated show of the season, "Dallas," probably had more than a little to do with that. Also, insiders reported that there was no love lost between Small and Brinkley. Small's remark, "I had hoped that David would stay with us for many more years," was not the type of comment one expects from a company eager to keep someone. Further eulogistic words from Small were: "It is like losing the home-run king. His departure from NBC News leaves a very big gap."

So David Brinkley retired in September.

In October, he unretired.

Although no one would confirm or deny the story, there were reports that during his last days at NBC, Brinkley had been deluged with offers from the other two networks and from Ted Turner, all anxious to get to Brinkley during that nether period between contract expiration and contract renewal. Whatever the circumstances, Brinkley announced early in October that he was joining ABC News. While turning down the spot as New York anchor (many felt Brinkley wasn't interested in sharing anchor duty; that was part of the reason he assumed the role as commentator when NBC brought in Chancellor), Brinkley expressed his desire to do a Sunday morning news program, on the order of "Meet the Press" or "Face the Nation." Roone Arledge immediately announced that Brinkley would host the new Sunday morning news program "This Week." A spokesman from NBC told *Time* magazine, "I do not know why NBC couldn't find a way to accomodate him. He is *the* most eminent newsman. It's crazy. You just don't throw away your most experienced reporter. Brinkley is the last of the great ones. . . ."

While NBC and ABC were trading Brinkley, CBS was capturing headlines with problems of its own. Their "60

Minutes," the prestigious Sunday evening show dedicated, it seemed at times, to reporting with an edge of scandal, found itself in the middle of a dandy. Morley Safer, apparently feeling the pressure from within, revealed to the press that the show had dropped plans to do a Safer story about poverty and political corruption in Haiti when Mike Wallace expressed concern that the story might cause members of his family located on the island some "problems." Don Hewitt, executive producer of "60 Minutes," announced immediately that the story on Haiti would indeed be produced. Originally scheduled for March 1981, as of August 1982 it still hadn't aired.

As if that cloud weren't enough, the "60 Minutes" cast and crew suffered another journalistic setback when the afternoon news program "Up to the Minute," produced by Hewitt and featuring the familiar faces of Wallace, Safer, Reasoner, and Bill Bradley, was canceled. Airing every day at 4:30 PM, "Up to the Minute" proved a ratings loser against the daytime barrage of soaps, games, and Mary Tyler Moore reruns. The reason for the failure of the show, according to CBS News, was the inordinate amount of time it demanded from the cohosts, time better spent on "60 Minutes." The impression given was that the reporter-hosts were personally involved with every aspect of the stories produced for the top-rated weekly show. This, too, was a notion that came under fire when Mike Wallace was accused of manipulating the facts of the story he did on General Westmoreland's behavior and tactics during the Vietnam War, a story the conservative *TV Guide* labeled a gross misrepresentation of the facts. These charges led to a deeper look at "60 Minutes," culminating with a report in *The New York Times* in which Wallace admitted that while he maintained hard and fast the integrity of all his stories, he thought it was fair to say that the amount of stories the show handled required a large production staff to go in ahead of the on-air reporter to do much of the research.

Perhaps the problems at "60 Minutes" had something to do with the sudden, unexpected decline in the "CBS Evening News with Dan Rather." Since his takeover, Rather's numbers simply weren't up to Cronkite's. This prompted the usual network reaction: resignation of a major executive. William Leonard announced his "retirement" as head of CBS News, effective spring 1982. Leonard had begun his network career with CBS in the early fifties as a news commentator, and had been a loyal employee since the early days of TV news broadcasting. His replacement was Van Gordon Sauter. Sauter announced that when he took over as head of CBS he would expand the morning news. The early morning network broadcast would begin at 7:00, making it directly competitive with "A.M. America" and "The Today Show." This meant, of course, that Bob Keeshan, better known as Captain Kangaroo, would be bumped ahead a half hour, from 7:00 to 6:30. Keeshan responded like the company man he was. He collapsed with a massive coronary.

Still more bad news was ahead for CBS. Walter Cronkite announced on October 16, 1981, that he was resigning from the board of directors of Pan American World Airways in order to remain free to cover aerospace stories for CBS News (while officially retired as the news anchor, Cronkite was still active, on a part-time basis, with CBS News, including a limited series about the universe reminiscent of his soft-news specials of the late fifties). On the surface, the story seemed harmless enough, but insiders knew what the implications of the announcement were. If the ratings of Dan Rather's Network News didn't improve, there was every possibility that Uncle Walter would be back at the helm, perhaps as nightly commentator, maybe even as the anchor. Ironically, it was John Chancellor, next in line to step down from long-term anchor duty who was now pulling in the big numbers at NBC.*

At NBC, the news of CBS's intention to muscle its morning operation, coupled with Brokaw's departure from "The Today Show," left a key slot open for replacement. The network announced in October—when it seemed as if all the announcements were being made—that it was going to replace Brokaw with two hosts instead of one, a continuation of the two-for-one plan for "Nightly News." Chris Wallace, the enthusiastic son of Mike Wallace, and Bryant Gumbel, a young, black sports reporter out of Los Angeles's NBC affiliate KNBC, were named as Brokaw's replacements. A great number of newscasters were rumored to have auditioned for the morning spot. How many? "Four," according to William Small.

In November, CBS announced that it was going to expand its evening news program to one hour. The reaction among the news faction at the network was immediate and positive. The reaction at the FCC was far less enthusiastic. The question was, how would the governmental regulatory agency react to the blatant violation of the 7:30 affiliate-designated half hour being reclaimed by the network? It was an academic question, because the affiliates balked at the idea first. The half-hour "community-interest" time-block had proved to be most profitable for the affiliates; they weren't that eager to give it up. No problem, according to the highest source at CBS, meaning William Paley. The affiliates were assured that they wouldn't lose any money, that CBS would compensate them for any drop in revenues. One estimate of how much CBS would have to compensate the affiliates went as high as fifty million dollars.

---

*By the fall of 1982, the "CBS Evening News" had recaptured a slim lead over ABC and NBC network news broadcast ratings.

One more point. Who was the best bet to be the anchor of a revamped one-hour nightly news program? Walter Cronkite.

Almost immediately, ABC and NBC announced that they, too, would expand their news coverage to sixty minutes. NBC, having already tried persuading the affiliates to go with an hour newcast, only to have the plan soundly rejected, now was able to use CBS for leverage, pointing out that failure to keep up would mean a ratings disaster —not for the news but for the entire prime-time schedule. Richard Wald, senior vice-president of ABC News, put it this way: "Of course we would like to be first. If someone else went first, we'd be a very quick second."

The affiliates, however, weren't so easily convinced. Phil Lombardo, president of the Corinthian stations (five of which were CBS affiliates) threatened to drop the CBS newscast entirely in favor of Ted Turner's new nightly half-hour news broadcast. In January, an informal poll of CBS affiliates showed that eighty-three were opposed to a one-hour news broadcast, twenty-one were enthusiastic, and ten had no opinion (the survey included about half the CBS affiliate stations).

"We have to have some fun doing this," Van Gordon Sauter proclaimed, once he took over CBS News. Almost immediately the fun began. Charles Kuralt was dismissed as the coanchor of "The CBS Morning News." Bill Kurtis, a forty-one-year-old CBS correspondent from Los Angeles before anchoring the local news at CBS affiliate WBBM in Chicago, was named as Kuralt's replacement. Kuralt's problems had begun shortly after he was arrested for drunken driving. Apparently, there was fun and there was fun. Kuralt was reassigned, put back "on the road" where, presumably, his driving record would improve.

A new producer was named for "The CBS Morning News," George Merlis, former producer of ABC's "Good

Morning America." While producing "Good Morning America," Merlis had done the impossible: he'd toppled "The Today Show" from its unshakeable post as the number-one morning network program, a spot held by the show for almost thirty years.

The best news program on the air in 1981 was, without question, ABC's "Nightline." Roone Arledge conceived "Nightline" in 1979 during the hostage crisis. When he wanted to do a late-night news operation, he was given an immediate go-ahead by the network. While heading ABC Sports, Arledge had received twenty-five Emmies, four Peabodys (the most distinguished award in television), and had been the executive producer of six Olympic broadcasts. Arledge introduced the idea of multiple anchors to the network news, attempting to match, kinetically, the pulse and rhythm of the events of the day with that of the broadcast. When he named Ted Koppel as host of the twenty-minute nightly report on the hostages, he gave America a new perspective on the possiblities of electronic journalism. Koppel was aggressive, short-tempered, articulate, and not afraid to show his impatience with guests who avoided his questions. He quickly established himself, often outranking the weary-looking Johnny Carson show on directly opposite Koppel. Based in Washington, "Nightline" soon became a five-nights-a-week, half-hour show, not afraid to handle any subject, often programming its subject matter cannily. The night John Belushi died was a Friday, an otherwise soft news day. The youth-oriented "Fridays" followed "Nightline." The choice was obvious to Arledge—Belushi was the subject with which "Nightline" should deal. When the Hinckley verdict was announced, "Nightline" scrubbed a scheduled report on the Middle East and, within three hours, went on the air with a brilliant half hour of news reporting dealing with the verdict. During the Falklands war, "Nightline" continually broke new ground, getting the most information directly to the American public before anyone else did.

Finally, Roone Arledge announced, in December 1981, that ABC had purchased 30 percent of UPI's TV news operation. UPITN, he said, owned 45 percent of the Independent Television News, a British nongovernment news operation. When the Falklands conflict exploded into war, ABC had the inside post. Luck? Perhaps. Know-how? Definitely. Instinct? Well, instinct is often the name of the game. And no one knows how to play it better than Roone Arledge.

14   Items—2

1. Who's who watching what.   The *New York Post* reported the viewing habits of the following celebrities: Rick Cerone, catcher for the New York Yankees, said that his favorite TV show was the afternoon soap opera "General Hospital." Jacqueline Bisset loves all interview shows. Helen Gurley Brown likes "The Today Show," "Phil Donahue," and "Dallas." Gil Gerard, TV's Buck Rogers, likes "Masterpiece Theatre." Jerry Falwell enjoys pro football, boxing, and the news.

2. Dallas.   "Dallas" made its debut in Japan, in February 1982. Although the Japanese had expressed a fondness in the past for American television, including such classics as "Charlie's Angels," "Columbo," and "Wagon Train," J.R. proved a little too much for the oriental audience to take. By March, Asahi National Broadcasting, the Japanese network carrying the show, began hinting at canceling the series. Victoria Principal was called up for tour duty to boost ratings, but the word, late in April, was that "Dallas" was slated for an early Japanese execution.

However, the Lorimar-produced series continued to be a smash hit in Marrakesh, Jakarta, and sixty-five other countries around the world carrying the show.

3. Washing dishes in public. The cable industry, fighting the big-dollar competition of the networks, found itself in the midst of another war—this one against dishes. The large, radarlike satellite-signal receivers were selling for upwards of five thousand dollars apiece, and the demand was, so far, outweighing the supply. The owner of a dish can receive virtually every TV broadcast, cablecast, and closed circuit signal sent from anywhere in the world. Even the pay-TV channels, including Home Box Office, Showtime, and Warner-Amex, were susceptible. The problem was a sticky one because no legislation existed to combat the problem. This was easy to understand, because prior to 1982, there wasn't any problem with which to contend. "A tempest in a teapot," said Peter Sutro, president of Cine-Tel Metroplex, one distributor of the dishes. Other prodish voices cried "restraint of trade." To further complicate matters, some purchasers of dishes (or groups of purchasers sharing the cost and use of the dishes) were sending checks to the various cable companies, in the hopes of avoiding protracted legal battles. The companies returned the checks uncashed, demanding that Congress clean up the dirty dishes.

It was interesting to watch the reaction among the cable operators. It hadn't been that long ago that they were on the other side of the fence, fighting the establishment networks for the right to carry network programming over the cable wires, a right which the FCC gave them.

Anyone familiar with the cable–network wars should have been well prepared for the FCC's decision on the legality of dish use. On June 23, 1982, the FCC approved the use of dishes for home use. Their reason was that the new equipment supplied areas with a clear transmission of the TV signal they previously couldn't receive. Direct Broadcast Satellite, or DBS, would allow the transmission of sports, entertainment, and news from anywhere in the world. Because of the high volume of equipment, the cost of the dishes was expected to fall dramatically, to approximately one hundred dollars a set. Leasing was also possible for as little as sixteen dollars a month, the cost of the average cable subscription with perhaps one pay-channel. Mark S. Fowler, chairman of the FCC, on what the decision would mean to local, affiliated stations, stated: "So long as there are people who want local news, who want to know what is going on in the region, the local stations will have a role. But it means they will have to serve the needs of their viewers if they want to stay viable." The FCC vote was 7–0 in favor of DBS.

4. Hold-out or holdup? As noted earlier, Suzanne Sommers staged one of the most publicized hold-outs of 1981, she was demanding $150,000 an episode. When the producers promptly fired her, Sommers found herself without a plot to kiss in.

John Schneider and Tom Wopat staged a boycott of "The Dukes of Hazzard," contending that they were being cheated out of their royalties from ancillary product sales related to the show. The producers, Warner Brothers TV, immediately began auditioning new actors to replace them. "The real star of the show is the Dodge charger, not the actors," one spokesman for the show said. Schneider and company sued the producers for thirty million dollars. The producers countersued for ninety million. Schneider and Wopat were eventually replaced. Put up your dukes.

The cast of "Dynasty," with the exception of John Forsythe, Linda Evans, and Joan Collins, was fired. The official word was that the show needed new faces. The unofficial word was that the cast had priced itself out of the market.

5. Television fights back.   U.S. Senator Paula Hawkins was knocked out by a TV studio backdrop that fell on her head during the taping of an interview. The Florida Republican was listed in fair condition and in good spirits.

6. Jim who?   Jim Aubrey, the controversial president of CBS-TV from 1959 through 1965, who was fired by William Paley over "personal differences" (low ratings), sold a TV show to—who else—CBS. "Shannon," on the fall 1981 schedule, was among the first shows canceled.

7. I don't know, what do you want to do?   Amidst all the strikes and protests among actors, producers, and Moral Majors, statistics showed that by far the most requested product for home-cassette viewing was X-rated movies. Better than 50 percent of all software sold was hard-core.

8. Where did I put Monday?   "Search for Tomorrow," TV's longest-running soap opera, produced and packaged by Procter and Gamble, found itself without a network for the first time in twenty-nine years. CBS decided to drop "Search" in favor of programming with a more "youthful" appeal; they chose a new soap, "The Young and the Restless," as the replacement. NBC promptly acquired "Search," scheduling it to run opposite its own replacement.

9. What next . . . ?   Public TV, under the gun because of federal cuts, announced that it was pursuing the possibility of selling commercial space to help pay its way. Jay Iselin, president of New York's popular Channel 13, one of the flagships of the Public Broadcasting System, made this startling comment: "We've seen what has happened to CBS, NBC, and ABC because they air advertising." Iselin went on to say, "Our commercials will creep onto the air so subtly our audience may not even notice them."

10. Professor Silverman. Fred Silverman announced that he would be teaching a course entitled "Television Programming, Today and Tomorrow" as a visiting professor at Syracuse University's School of Public Communications in January 1982. Silverman must have done well at Syracuse. In June 1982, it was announced that he'd made it to the pilot stage of a new series, "Farrell for the People." The made-for-TV movie was put together by MGM and Silverman's new, independent production company, Inter Media.

11. Assassination. One evening early in the season, Johnny Carson taped "The Tonight Show" in Burbank, as usual, and left the studios at 7:00 PM. A little later that night, one Cary Blue Stilfield walked onto the empty "Tonight Show" set and proceeded to blast it with his shotgun. Arrested a short time later, Stilfield explained to authorities that he didn't like television and was trying to take care of the problem.

12. Which Wallace was that? Mike Wallace, investigating a San Diego Savings and Loan fraud specializing in low-income victims, was reportedly asked why the victims would sign contracts without reading them. "They're probably too busy eating their watermelon and tacos," Wallace replied. It was a very long year for the veteran "60 Minutes" reporter.

13. General Hospital. I hurt my leg while in Los Angeles and had to go to a doctor. I made an appointment with a Beverly Hills foot specialist. When I arrived at his office, I had to wait with several other people until my turn came. Instead of magazines, there was a huge color

TV in the waiting room. Everyone was glued to the set, watching "General Hospital."

14. Where's Johnny?   It just wasn't Johnny Carson's year. He was arrested in the spring of 1982 for drunken driving. The same night, F. Lee Bailey was also arrested for the same offense, near San Francisco. When Johnny returned to "The Tonight Show," an actor dressed as a police officer appeared with him. Johnny asked permission from the cop to do his monologue. The cop/actor nodded, the audience roared. Johnny attributed the nationwide headlines of his arrest to the fact that "it was a slow news weekend. And what luck: My lawyer's F. Lee Bailey."

15. That's not real spaghetti sauce if it comes from a jar.   A research report, issued by the Commission for Social Justice, a group aligned with the Order of the Sons of Italy, once again raised a brouhaha over the way Italians were being portrayed on television. (The last time this happened, all Italians disappeared from crime shows. Most notably, Al Capone, in an "Untouchables" episode, seemed to be of Greek descent.)

The findings of the Committee:

Negative Italo-American portrayls outnum-
    bered positive depictions two to one.
Most Italo-Americans didn't speak proper En-
    glish on TV.
Most had low-status jobs.
Most were male.

No one seemed to remember Frank Furillo of "Hill Street Blues." Anyway, no one speaks proper English on TV. The real point is that pressure tactics were now commonplace as the networks scrambled to please everyone, producing a roster of programming by committee, and resulting in a perpetuation of the mythic rootless American cartoon of humanity that, rather than celebrating its ethnicity, vehemently denies it.

16. I love New York, even if it has pigeons. NBC's "Love, Sidney," a favorite target of The Coalition for Better Television, was finally kicked out of New York, but not by Jerry Falwell or the Reverend Wildmon. The dirty deed was done by Big Bird of Sesame Street. Tony Randall and Swoosie Kurtz, the stars of "Love, Sidney," had clauses in their contracts that guaranteed that the show would be taped in New York. However, the only available space was previously committed to "Sesame Street." So, for eight episodes "Love, Sidney" moved to the West Coast while Big Bird learned the alphabet.

Upon their return to New York, Randall and Kurtz were accorded a personal welcome by Mayor Koch. It was as if the fleet had returned. In many ways, it had. "Love, Sidney" was the networks' favorite reason for denying the seriousness of the coalition's efforts, even as NBC continued to hold the reins on Sydney's sexual preferences. The result: just another widow-father/parentless niece sit-com. The victory went to Wildmon after all.

17. Gary, please don't grow. NBC got the jitters when its biggest (and smallest) star, Gary Coleman, developed kidney troubles shortly after coming to terms with the network. His first kidney transplant, nine years ago, was now being rejected by his body. After extensive medical treatment, doctors gave Gary the go-ahead to return to work. But, horror of horrors!—Gary started growing again, up from his three-foot ten-inch arrested development, a side-effect of his previous drug regimen. The fear that Gary's improving health might prove fatal to "Diff'rent Strokes" caused much anxiety at NBC. The show was one of the few hits the network had.

18. Take it easy, Fiji. They have European sports and electronic games, Asian movies, exotic menus. They have rock and roll, sophisticated sound equipment, and lots of candy. However, the 700,000 inhabitants of Fiji don't have television, and they're starting to get a little perturbed about it. The Fiji government announced that the introduction of television broadcasting, scheduled to begin early in 1981, would be delayed "until the people are ready for it."

Not to worry. Videotape machines on the island sell for approximately $1,800, the average annual income. Nearby Suva is much more fortunate. They not only have TV, they've got "Charlie's Angels" and "Saturday Night Live," their two favorite programs. The government is reportedly concerned.

19. Postmortems. As the 1981–1982 season faded into memory, the lingering shock of John Belushi's death was kept alive by the now harrowing syndicated reruns of "Saturday Night Live," seen in most markets five nights a week. The personal struggles of Belushi, a sensation of television and a flop in the movies (only one of his seven films was a money-maker—*Animal House*) reminded those who cared about the talented performer that an actor's success forces a trade-off: the public's curiosity for the right to privacy.

One death overlooked by most of the media was that of Hugh Beaumont, a clergyman turned actor who played the stern father in the neoclassic fifties sit-com "Leave it to Beaver." He was seventy-two, a father-figure for the post-war baby boom set, TV's first generation.

The death of Harvey Lembeck at the age of fifty-eight was, perhaps, the saddest. Lembeck, who rose to fame in the fifties as one of the prisoners in the feature film *Stalag 17* and then played Phil Silvers's sidekick in the "Sergeant Bilko" series, was something of a legend in Hollywood. In the late seventies he formed a comedy school for professional actors and actresses. His classes were the most respected, revered workshops in town.

My most vivid memory of Lembeck was seeing him and saying hello in the juice bar of the health club to which we both belonged in Beverly Hills. There he would sit, day after day, fat, wrinkled, lonely, telling whomever walked by about some new project he was working on, some "hot" film he was up for and sure to get. Friends would listen, pat him on the back, and move on. He was a performer without a stage. Just waiting, waiting, waiting. . . .

15 The Ratings—3

CBS managed to edge out ABC in the November sweeps. It was, however, a qualified victory. By the end of the first half of the season the overall share of the three networks combined was down nearly nine points over the preceding five-year period and three full points over the past year alone. Further, not one of the nearly two dozen new shows was a smash. Most, in fact, were on the cancellation block, if not already off the air.

The positive side of the picture was that more hardware—TVs, video projectors, and VCRs—was being sold. Overall network advertising revenues in 1981 exceeded $5.5 billion. Also, in spite of the fact that fewer people were watching the big three, viewing time was up: 6.7 hours a day in the average home.

One highly credible advertising agency conducted an independent survey for the networks that reported a fifteenfold increase in subscriptions to pay-cable in the previous twelve months. The report concluded with a prediction, based on these figures, that overall network shares would continue to decline by as much as twelve more points, down to 71 percent of the present viewing audience by 1985, 59 percent by 1990.

The report confirmed what the networks already knew. Network success ratios had been adjusted in 1981 to account for the viewer attrition. The success barometer had stood at a 30 share for years. Now it was reduced to a 26 share for survival. Some network shows were qualified hits with as little as 24 percent of the viewing audience tuning in.

The following is a complete listing of the first half of the 1981–1982 season ratings of the three major networks:

RANK	SERIES	AVERAGE	1980–1981
1.	"Dallas" (CBS)	28.1	31.8
2.	"60 Minutes" (CBS)	27.6	26.8
3.	"M*A*S*H" (CBS)	23.0	23.5
4.	"The Jeffersons" (CBS)	22.7	21.9
	"Alice" (CBS)	22.7	21.5
6.	"One Day at a Time" (CBS)	22.3	21.1
7.	"Three's Company" (ABC)	22.2	21.0
8.	"Dukes of Hazzard" (CBS)	21.8	25.2
	"NFL Monday Night Football (ABC)†	21.8	20.1
10.	"Archie Bunker's Place" (CBS)	21.4	20.3
11.	"Too Close for Comfort" (ABC)	21.2	20.6
	"Happy Days" (ABC)	21.2	20.1
13.	"Love Boat" (ABC)	21.0	24.1
14.	"Trapper John, M.D." (CBS)	20.9	20.0

†Currently off schedule.

RANK	SERIES	AVERAGE	1980–1981
15.	"ABC Sunday Movie"	20.5	20.6
16.	"Laverne and Shirley" (ABC)	20.2	19.9
17.	"Hart to Hart" (ABC)	20.1	18.7
18.	"Little House on the Prairie" (NBC)	19.8	21.6
19.	"Bret Maverick" (NBC)	19.6	—
20.	"House Calls" (CBS)	19.5	22.3
21.	"Magnum, P.I." (CBS)	19.4	20.9
22.	"Dynasty" (ABC)	19.2	19.0
	"Falcon Crest" (CBS)	19.2	—
24.	"The Fall Guy" (ABC)	18.9	—
	"Hill Street Blues" (NBC)	18.9	13.3
26.	"NBC Monday Movies"	18.7	18.0
	"That's Incredible" (ABC)	18.7	19.8
28.	"Facts of Life" (NBC)	18.6	18.7
	"Real People" (NBC)	18.6	21.3
30.	"Fantasy Island" (ABC)	18.4	20.1
31.	"Lou Grant" (CBS)	17.7	19.0
32.	"Father Murphy" (NBC)	17.6	—
	"Love, Sidney" (NBC)	17.6	—
34.	"Private Benjamin" (CBS)	17.5	23.9
	"The Incredible Hulk" (CBS)*	17.5	16.9
36.	"Today's FBI" (ABC)	17.2	—
37.	"Mork and Mindy" (ABC)	17.1	16.9
	"The Greatest American Hero" (ABC)	17.1	21.1
39.	"Quincy" (NBC)	16.8	18.2
	"Barney Miller" (ABC)	16.8	18.4
41.	"Mr. Merlin" (CBS)	16.7	—
	"CHiPs" (NBC)	16.7	19.4
43.	"Knots Landing" (CBS)	16.6	18.8
	"Diff'rent Strokes" (NBC)	16.6	20.5

*Canceled.

RANK	*SERIES*	*AVERAGE*	*1980–1981*
45.	"Walt Disney" (CBS)	16.4	15.3
	"Barbara Mandrell" (NBC)	16.4	16.6
	"CBS Saturday Movies"	16.4	13.8
48.	"WKRP in Cincinnati" (CBS)	15.9	16.9
49.	"Best of the West" (ABC)	15.8	—
50.	"Benson" (ABC)	15.7	16.0
	"CBS Tuesday Movies"	15.7	17.1
	"Taxi" (ABC)	15.7	16.7
53.	"The Two of Us" (CBS)	15.6	21.6
54.	"NBC Sunday Movies"	15.5	—
55.	"Gimme a Break" (NBC)	15.3	—
56.	"20/20" (ABC)	14.4	17.3
57.	"Bosom Buddies" (ABC)	14.3	17.3
58.	"Nurse" (CBS)	14.1	17.3
59.	"Flamingo Road" (NBC)	13.7	16.7
60.	"Simon and Simon" (CBS)	13.3	—
61.	"Jessica Novak" (CBS)*	13.2	—
	"Code Red" (ABC)	13.2	—
63.	"Harper Valley" (NBC)	13.1	17.0
64.	"Nashville Palace" (NBC)*	12.7	—
	"McClain's Law" (NBC)	12.7	—
	"Here's Boomer" (NBC)	12.7	—
	"CBS Wednesday Movie"	12.7	16.9
68.	"The Flintstones" (NBC)†	12.6	12.6
69.	"NBC Tuesday Movies"†	12.5	—
70.	"Making a Living" (ABC)*	12.4	18.0
71.	"Strike Force" (ABC)	12.3	—
	"Maggie" (ABC)*	12.3	—
73.	"Darkroom" (ABC)*	12.0	—
74.	"NBC Friday Movies"†	11.6	12.2
75.	"Shannon" (CBS)†	11.5	—
76.	"Open All Night" (ABC)	11.4	—

*Canceled.
†Currently off schedule.

RANK	SERIES	AVERAGE	1980–1981
77.	"NBC Magazine"	11.2	8.1
78.	"Lewis and Clark" (NBC)*	10.5	—
79.	"Television: Inside and Out" (NBC)*	10.4	—
80.	"Fitz and Bones" (NBC)*	8.7	—
81.	"NBC Saturday Movies"†	8.2	13.7

*Canceled.
†Currently off schedule.

CBS won the first half-season with a 19.7 overall rating. ABC registered with a close 18.4, while NBC limped along with 15.5.

If any of the new crop of shows could be called a success it would have to be "Falcon Crest," a mimeograph of "Dallas," that followed the successful Texas-based evening soap opera in the schedule. The huge lead-in audience insured the continuing saga of a wine family's adventures a solid ratings base.

At NBC, the new shows, with younger, unknown stars, were continually outperforming the "retreads," including "Bret Maverick" and "McClain's Law," two of the bigger disappointments of the 1981–1982 season. The most optimistic NBC could get was over the modified success of "Love, Sidney," in spite of Reverend Wildmon singling out the show as particularly repugnant to the members of The Coalition for Better Television. On the down-side, the bottom five shows of the half-season all belonged to NBC.

At ABC, the only unqualified hit of the new entires was "The Fall Guy," starring Lee Majors as a stuntman doubling as a private investigator for hire.

With the new year, the second half of the TV season brought along the schedule changes from the networks:

	7:30	8:00	8:30
MONDAY	(Local)	That's Incredible	
	(Local)	Mr. Merlin	Private Benjamin
	(Local)	Little House on the Prairie	
TUESDAY	(Local)	Happy Days	Laverne & Shirley
	(Local)	Simon & Simon	
	(Local)	Father Murphy	
WEDNESDAY	(Local)	The Greatest American Hero	
	(Local)	WKRP in Cincinnati	The Two of Us
	(Local)	Real People	
THURSDAY	(Local)	Mork & Mindy	Best of the West
	(Local)	Magnum, P.I.	
	(Local)	FAME	
FRIDAY	(Local)	Benson	Bosom Buddies
	(Local)	The Dukes of Hazzard	
	(Local)	NBC Magazine	
SATURDAY	(Local)	KING'S CROSSING	
	(Local)	Walt Disney	
	(Local)	ONE OF THE BOYS	Harper Valley

	7:00	7:30	8:00	8:30
SUNDAY	Code Red		Today's FBI	
	60 Minutes		Archie Bunker's Place	One Day at a Time
	PEACOCK SHOWCASE		Chips	

9:00	9:30	10:00	10:30	
MOVIE				ABC
M*A*S*H	House Calls	Lou Grant		CBS
Movie				NBC

9:00	9:30	10:00	10:30	
Three's Company	Too Close for Comfort	Hart to Hart		ABC
Movie				CBS
Bret Maverick		Flamingo Road		NBC

9:00	9:30	10:00	10:30	
The Fall Guy		Dynasty		ABC
MOVIE				CBS
Facts of Life	Love, Sidney	Quincy		NBC

9:00	9:30	10:00	10:30	
Barney Miller	Taxi	20/20		ABC
Knots Landing		Nurse		CBS
Diff'rent Strokes	Gimme a Break	Hill Street Blues		NBC

9:00	9:30	10:00	10:30	
Darkroom		Strike Force		ABC
Dallas		Falcon Crest		CBS
McClain's Law		CASSIE and CO.		NBC

9:00	9:30	10:00	10:30	
Love Boat		Fantasy Island		ABC
Movie				CBS
Barbara Mandrell		DEVLIN CONNECTION		NBC

9:00	9:30	10:00	10:30	
Movie				ABC
Alice	The Jeffersons	Trapper John, M.D.		CBS
Movie				NBC

ABC: "Open All Night" and "Making a Living" were canceled; "King's Crossing" was added to the lineup.

NBC: "Television: Inside and Out" with Rona Barrett, "Lewis and Clark," and "One of the Boys" were all canceled. "The Devlin Connection" was removed from the schedule due to Rock Hudson's health problems. "Cassie and Company," starring Angie Dickinson and produced by Johnny Carson Productions, was tentatively scheduled for a Thursday slot.

CBS: The only change here was the addition of a movie to the Wednesday schedule.

16 Executive Actions

The last time we left Tom Snyder, we were left with Tom Snyder, Rona Barrett having departed from "The Tomorrow Show" and, shortly thereafter, from "The Today Show." In her wake, Tom seemed to float along with a grin of victory.

That grin soon faded, along with "The Tomorrow Show" itself. With Miss Rona absent from duty, the ratings began to plummet lower than ever before. Once again, the strength of late-night programming demonstrated the theory of lead-in strength. The surging "Nightline" on ABC was keeping viewers with reruns of "The Love Boat" and other late-night alternatives to Johnny and his band of merry pranksters. The clincher came for Snyder when Fred Silverman officially left the network in June 1981. Everyone knew that Tom was one of Silverman's favorites, that there was even talk, way back when Silverman first came to NBC that, perhaps, Snyder was the right fellow to replace one of Silverman's "enemies," Johnny Carson.

Grant Tinker, though, had other ideas. Whereas Silverman was, like Snyder, a *mensch,* Tinker was decidedly the patrician, public television personality with a commercial appetite. Almost as soon as he was enthroned, Tinker made his intentions known. He told *TV Guide:* "I really think . . . to do a better job of programming, TV should aim at more difficult targets; make more 'Lou Grants' and fewer 'Lobos.' " There was no doubt about where Snyder fit in this schema. He was decidedly more Lobo than Lou.

Having served as an NBC programmer from 1961 through 1967, Tinker knew enough about the business of television to understand the distribution of power. It was obvious to him that Silverman's downfall was due, at least in part, to his insisting on taking all the chances, calling all the shots, wearing the high profile, and, ultimately, falling flat on his well-publicized face. Tinker was not about to set himself up in front of a crowd, only to be caught with his ratings down. The first move Tinker made, once he returned to NBC, was to install Brandon Tartikoff as the head of programming. Tartikoff, on the other hand, was decidedly in the public eye, with the personality to go with it. He was the *Playboy* ideal of a young executive, with one foot on the corporate ladder and the other on the exercise bike pedal.

Tartikoff, like Tinker, was not a fan of "The Tomorrow Show," nor its boozy, barroom atmosphere of cigarettes, ego, and wisecrackery. The end lurked nearer after Snyder's disastrous interview with Charles Manson, late in 1981. The piece was unbelievably dull; Manson easily dominated Snyder, who seemed totally at a loss with one of the most sought-after subjects in the past decade. It wasn't long after the Manson show that NBC announced that it was going to shave a half hour from the ninety-minute "Tomorrow Show," restoring it to its original sixty-minute length. All right, Snyder could live with that.

The killer, though, was that the show was to be

pushed back another full hour, so that its starting time would be 1:30 in the morning. Moreover, David Letterman, another up-and-coming Carson, was going to get the 12:30–1:30 slot. As early as October, the smart money said Snyder would be gone before Christmas.

Sure enough, on November 5, Tom Snyder announced that he was quitting "The Tomorrow Show." The announcement came after Snyder met face to face with Tartikoff, in what informed sources reported was a futile last-minute plea by Snyder to keep his 12:30 time-slot.

Letterman was the "darling" of the new regime. Tinker and Tartikoff had seen his early-morning live program of a year and a half ago, another failed Silverman experiment. Now that Silverman's bathwater had been discarded, Letterman was Tinker's baby. He was kept on the NBC payroll at a reported two hundred thousand dollars a year, so that he couldn't go anywhere else. Finally, NBC was happy to announce that, starting in February, "The David Letterman Show," live from New York, would make its debut Monday through Thursday, 12:30–1:30 A.M.

Tom Snyder walked off his show and into the ether of reruns from November to February only to return to local news anchor in late August, for ABC's New York local O and O flagship.

The Phil Donahue escape from NBC was yet another in a series of talk-show cancellations that occurred in 1981. When the smoke cleared, the only show that remained unscathed was "The Tonight Show." Even though the show was trimmed to one hour, it was done so at Carson's insistence. However, the rundown of the rest of the crop reads like a hit-list. There is the above-mentioned departure of Rona and Tom from "The Tomorrow Show." Merv Griffin cut his show back to an hour, and was steadily losing affiliates. Mike Douglas was canceled. He found work, *sans* band and audience, replacing Lee Leonard (also canceled) on Ted Turner's Cable News Network, doing late-night celebrity interviews. John Davidson, Mike Douglas's replacement on the Westinghouse talk-show circuit, was canceled. Regis Philbin's early-morning network show for NBC lasted about thirty commercial breaks before it, too, bit the dust. Philbin was another in a long line of also-rans who found temporary shelter in cable. Philbin's oasis was the Health Channel, where he was recruited to host what would amount to a series of exercise and diet tips.

For commercial TV, though, the talk-show syndrome had, for the moment, run out of breath. Could David Letterman be the future of TV chatter? We'll find out after a word from the sponsors.

17 Moral Majors—2

Toward the end of January, the Reverend Donald Wildmon announced yet another boycott of products that were advertised on shows the coalition found objectionable. The target date for the boycott was March 2. The target group was "those shows that emphasize excessive sex, violence and profanity, as well as anti-Christian bigotry." This last issue was a new flap, more than just an expansion of goals. It marked the formal split between Wildmon and Falwell.

Falwell came out of the summer and fall vigilantism somewhat less than morally uplifted. For one thing, his Sunday sermons were losing ratings and revenues. The effectiveness of Reverend Wildmon seemed to have been damaged by the continual "cry wolf" pattern of yes-a-boycott/no-a-boycott flip-flopping, and what Falwell perceived as a generally ineffective attempt to manipulate the curious, the threatened, and the true believers. Falwell decided to align himself more closely with Richard Viguerie, the political arm of the Moral Majority, while easing up on the Elmer Gantry theatrics.

To make his position known to the public, Falwell, in the first in a series of fence-mending (or face-saving) gestures, declared, "Our feeling [the Moral Majority's] is that the networks have made a significant effort to clean up their act."

Falwell wasn't the only one to respond to Wildmon. Whereas terror tactics at the top of the season had sent the networks into a panic, the urgent issues of declining audiences and the threat of cable TV had taken the thunder out of Wildmon's storm of protest. Said one advertising spokesman: "I don't think there is much expectation that any boycott would be successful." Added another: "I don't think companies are being intimidated. But they're careful, and they're concerned about the public relations of being targeted. Some advertisers are avoiding serials like 'Dallas' and 'Flamingo Road,' which have the most sex, and shows like 'Strike Force' with a lot of violence." Maybe so, but the shows were top rated, and if there is one thing more divine than righteousness, it is ratings. By the end of the season, all three shows were selling out their available space.

Grant Tinker, unlike Fred Silverman, wasn't afraid to take on the Reverend Wildmon in public. In fact, he used Wildmon's attacks to further his own desires to upgrade the quality of TV: "If we did better programs, just higher quality television, the questions about content would go away. Our big sin, if one is being committed, is not the level of sex or violence in shows, but the lowest-common-denominator phenomenon, the fact that we're not producing better shows. I think he's picking on the wrong evil."

Jerry Falwell wasn't the only member of the coalition to see the handwriting on the wall. The Christian Broadcasting Network was praying for a miracle as 1982 brought the hard facts of life to such ventures as "Another Life," a soap opera produced by the CBN. The networks gave the show a daytime slot, either out of fear or to see just how powerful Wildmon's following was. The show was offered under a barter system, wherein a station gets the show for free and shares in the revenues of the sponsorship, in this case donations. Before the end of its first season, however, the show's affiliate network had dwindled from sixty stations to forty-five, most of them on the UHF band. Here is a typical plot line and dramatic moment from "Another Life:" One of the stars, a typical no-good daytime type, is in the hospital suffering from a heart attack, or maybe cancer. The good doctors tell him it's all over. Wait, though, there is one thing left! Pray, pray to Jesus!! Cut to a ray of light on the victim's face, and he's cured!

The boycott never came off.

Meanwhile, Ed Asner, the Moral Major of the left, was continuing to make some very secular noise all his own. He announced his intention, in the fall of 1981, to run against incumbent William Schallert for the presidency of the Screen Actors Guild. Asner's platform was built on the dissatisfaction he expressed with the Guild's acceptance of the settlement the year before, a settlement he felt hadn't benefited Guild members enough.

The campaign was a particularly bitter one, with both sides hurling invective like pies in a slapstick comedy. Finally, it came down to the voting. Asner received 9,689 votes to Schallert's 7,188. A third candidate, Morgan Paull, received 1,197 votes. Asner was elated. At his acceptance ceremony, he said the victory was only the beginning. He would work to achieve a merger with the American Federation of Television and Radio Artists (AFTRA) and the Screen Extras Guild (SEG). It was Asner's intended goal to merge with all of the Hollywood guilds and unions, combining actors, writers, directors, and technicians into one mighty force, to turn the wheel of power toward unionism rather than management.

If Asner was full of hope and optimism, he soon found

himself embroiled in what was to be one of the bitterest controversies to come out of Hollywood since the early fifties. In February, Asner headed a group of actors who donated a total $25,000 to buy medical supplies for the guerrillas in El Salvador. This set off a wave of fury among the more conservative elements of the union, headed by former SAG president Charlton Heston. Heston was seething with anger over what he perceived as Asner's attempts to repoliticize the Screen Actors Guild. In March, Asner stated publicly that the union ought to capitalize on its strength by endorsing political candidates as a way of helping the guild to attain better working conditions and more money.

Heston called Asner's comments "out of line." Asner's reply will go down in Hollywood's history as the infamous Cocksucker Incident. By referring to Heston as "that cocksucker," Asner succeeded in weakening his own position of authority. "Reagan's stooge" was another epithet Asner tossed Heston's way. "Old-time Tammany Hall tactics, including arm-twisting," was the way Heston described Asner's union organizing. If all these expressions, with the possible exception of the cocksucker statement, sounded more political than thespian, it may have been because Asner seemed, as did his Moral Major mirror, Jerry Falwell, to be on the springboard of a political career.

Asner, in late March, was working toward merger between SAG and SEG. Heston and Robert Conrad organized the conservative wing of SAG to defeat the merger. They claimed, among other things, that such a merger would only create greater hardships for SAG members, opening the door to ever-increasing competition while possibly forcing actors to accept work as extras. Finally, in early May, with fewer than twenty thousand of the Guild's fifty thousand members voting, the merger was defeated. Although it received a 58 percent majority of the vote, it needed 60 percent to win. The next day, Asner got the Guild's national board to reintroduce the merger plan for a vote the following season—after the local Los Angeles board voted a stunning 20–0 against such a move. Much bitterness was expressed toward Asner, who in turn accused the right-wing faction of the Guild of confusing the issues of political support and union merger.

On the eve of the summer hiatus, the word came from CBS that "Lou Grant" was canceled. The network insisted the show was being canceled because of poor ratings. Asner insisted the show was dropped because he was the target of fifties-style blacklisting. As to whether or not Lou Grant's show was actually a victim of blacklisting, it's extremely hard to prove. Asner's Q rating had certainly plunged as word spread of his unfortunate choice of words. Yet "Lou Grant" wasn't the only long-run show that was coming to an end. Also targeted for cancellation were CBS's "WKRP in Cincinnati" and ABC's "Taxi" and "Barney Miller." Even "M*A*S*H" announced that it would do one more half-season and call it quits.

" 'Lou Grant' was the only issue-oriented drama on television," Ed Asner announced. "I find it shallow that the network wouldn't have exerted itself on behalf of the show, especially so that the yahoos of the world couldn't claim another victory in their attempt to abridge free speech."

James Rosenfield, executive vice-president of CBS, claimed that Asner's political statements and politics in general had no bearing on the cancellation of "Lou Grant." Rosenfield went on to say that the show got "heavier and heavier" at a time when "audience trends" were toward lighter fare and escapist programming.

And yet, and yet. A couple of years ago, Lee Grant's TV series "Fay" was canceled after only two weeks on the air. Grant had been among the fringe of the blacklisted crowd who'd found it more difficult than most to get regular series duty. When she got her shot, she was removed immediately as it came time to decide whether or not to try and save her show from instant oblivion. Mickey Rooney's "One of the Boys" was canceled shortly after he announced a major lawsuit against the networks for playing his pre-1948 films without his permission—a challenge to the old agreement that formed the basis of the SAG and WGA series of strikes concerning future royalties from cable and cassette.

At the same time, such apolitical fluff as "Taxi" was no sooner canceled from ABC, than NBC and HBO were bidding for the rights to keep the show alive in prime time. NBC prevailed, slotting "Taxi" into its fall schedule.

If the substance wasn't totally there for Asner's cries of "foul," at least a shadow still lingered.

18 The Ratings—4

The season was coming to an end with CBS clearly the winner in the ratings race. In February 1982, the second sweeps month, CBS held a commanding 19.3 weekly season average to ABC's 17.6 and NBC's struggling 16.5. In terms of the "second season" averages, meaning the weeks following the November sweeps, the numbers were CBS 19.5, ABC 17.9, NBC. 15.4.

However, the networks, while satisfied with the lack of any further fall-off, were startled by a demographic breakdown that showed that teenagers were defecting from the television screen in favor of other forms of entertainment—principally electronic games and movies. This news was cause for concern, because during the past decade the principal source of revenue, and therefore the principal target of programming, was the twelve- to eighteen-year-old age bracket.

The networks, once firmly anchored in spring production shut-downs after the February sweeps, were gearing up for what was now referred to along TV Row as "the third season." ABC, seeing itself in a two-way

	7:30	8:00	8:30
MONDAY	(Local)	That's Incredible	
	(Local)	Private Benjamin	REPORT TO MURPHY
	(Local)	Little House on the Prairie	

	7:30	8:00	8:30
TUESDAY	(Local)	Happy Days	JOANIE LOVES CHACHI
	(Local)	Q.E.D.	
	(Local)	Bret Maverick	

	7:30	8:00	8:30
WEDNESDAY	(Local)	The Greatest American Hero	
	(Local)	HERBIE THE LOVE BUG	
	(Local)	Real People	

	7:30	8:00	8:30
THURSDAY	(Local)	NO SOAP, RADIO	Mork & Mindy
	(Local)	Magnum, P.I.	
	(Local)	Fame	

	7:30	8:00	8:30
FRIDAY	(Local)	Benson	Barney Miller
	(Local)	The Dukes of Hazzard	
	(Local)	JOKEBOOK	

	7:30	8:00	8:30
SATURDAY	(Local)	T.J. HOOKER	
	(Local)	Walt Disney	
	(Local)	Harper Valley	One of the Boys

	7:00	7:30	8:00	8:30
SUNDAY	INSIDE AMERICA		Today's FBI	
	60 Minutes		Archie Bunker's Place	One Day at a Time
	Father Murphy		Chips	

9:00	9:30	10:00	10:30	
Movie				ABC
M*A*S*H	MAKING THE GRADE	Lou Grant		CBS
Movie				NBC

9:00	9:30	10:00	10:30	
Three's Company	Too Close for Comfort	Hart to Hart		ABC
Movie				CBS
Flamingo Road		SHAPE OF THINGS		NBC

9:00	9:30	10:00	10:30	
The Fall Guy		Dynasty		ABC
WKRP in Cincinnati	BAKER'S DOZEN	Shannon		CBS
Facts of Life	TEACHERS ONLY	Quincy		NBC

9:00	9:30	10:00	10:30	
9 TO 5	Taxi	20/20		ABC
Simon & Simon		Knots Landing		CBS
Diff'rent Strokes	Gimme a Break	Hill Street Blues		NBC

9:00	9:30	10:00	10:30	
THE PHOENIX		Strike Force		ABC
Dallas		Nurse		CBS
Chicago Story		McClain's Law		NBC

9:00	9:30	10:00	10:30	
Love Boat		Fantasy Island		ABC
Movie				CBS
Barbara Mandrell		NBC Magazine		NBC

9:00	9:30	10:00	10:30	
Movie				ABC
Alice	The Jeffersons	Trapper John, M.D.		CBS
Movie				NBC

dogfight, was determined to pull strong figures for the upcoming May sweeps, the next ratings month that "counted." The network put eight new shows onto its schedule.

One of the new eight, "Joanie Loves Chachi," premiered at number one in the ratings. It was the latest in the Garry Marshall plan for programming dominance. Pages 170–171 list the complete third season schedule:

Finally, here are the rankings of all the TV shows for the 1981–1982 season, in descending order. The ratings are seasonal averages. Shows that were canceled, or that had a preset limited-run are so indicated.

RANK	SERIES	RATING
1.	"Dallas" (CBS)	28.4
2.	"60 Minutes" (CBS)	27.7
3.	"Jeffersons" (CBS)	23.4
4.	"Joanie Loves Chachi" (ABC)†	23.3
	"Three's Company" (ABC)	23.3
6.	"Alice" (CBS)	22.7
7.	"Dukes of Hazzard" (CBS)	22.6
	"Too Close for Comfort" (ABC)	22.6
9.	"ABC Monday Movie"*	22.5
10.	"M*A*S*H" (CBS)	22.3
11.	"One Day at a Time" (CBS)	22.0
12.	"NFL Monday Football" (ABC)	21.8
13.	"Archie Bunker's Place" (CBS)	21.6
14.	"Falcon Crest" (CBS)	21.4
15.	"Love Boat" (ABC)	21.2
16.	"Hart to Hart" (ABC)	21.1
	"Trapper John, M.D." (CBS)	21.1
18.	"Magnum, P.I." (CBS)	20.9
19.	"Happy Days" (ABC)	20.6
20.	"Dynasty" (ABC)	20.2

†Five airings or fewer.
*Canceled.

RANK	SERIES	RATING
21.	"Laverne and Shirley" (ABC)	19.9
22.	"Real People" (NBC)	19.7
23.	"ABC Sunday Movie"	19.5
24.	"House Calls" (CBS)*	19.2
25.	"Facts of Life" (NBC)	19.1
	"Little House on the Prairie" (NBC)	19.1
27.	"Fall Guy" (ABC)	19.0
28.	"Hill Street Blues" (NBC)	18.6
29.	"That's Incredible" (ABC)	18.4
	"T.J. Hooker" (ABC)†	18.4
31.	"Fantasy Island" (ABC)	18.3
32.	'"NBC Monday Movie"	18.1
33.	"9 to 5" (ABC)†	17.9
34.	"Bret Maverick" (NBC)*	17.7
35.	"Incredible Hulk" (CBS)†*	17.5
	"Diff'rent Strokes" (NBC)	17.5
37.	"Private Benjamin" (CBS)	17.3
38.	"Making the Grade" (CBS)†*	17.1
39.	"Love, Sidney" (NBC)	17.0
40.	"Knots Landing" (CBS)	16.9
41.	"CHiPs" (NBC)	16.7
	"Mr. Merlin" (CBS)*	16.7
43.	"Lou Grant" (CBS)*	16.6
	"The Greatest American Hero" (ABC)	16.6
45.	"Quincy" (NBC)	16.5
	"Teachers Only" (NBC)†	16.5
	"Gimme a Break" (NBC)	16.5
48.	"Today's FBI" (ABC)	16.3
	"Walt Disney" (CBS)	16.3
	"CBS Saturday Movie"	16.3
51.	"NBC Sunday Movie"	16.1

†Five airings or fewer.
*Canceled.

RANK	SERIES	RATING
52.	"Father Murphy" (NBC)	15.9
53.	"Taxi" (ABC)*	15.8
54.	"Barney Miller" (ABC)*	15.7
55.	"Report to Murphy" (CBS)†*	15.6
	"WKRP in Cincinnati" (CBS)*	15.6
57.	"Police Squad" (ABC)†*	15.5
58.	"CBS Wednesday Movie"*	15.4
	"Nurse" (CBS)*	15.4
60.	"20/20" (ABC)	15.3
	"Morky and Mindy" (ABC)	15.3
	"Two of Us" (CBS)*	15.3
63.	"Benson" (ABC)	15.2
	"Cagney and Lacey" (CBS)†	15.2
65.	"Fame" (NBC)	15.1
66.	"Herbie, the Love Bug" (CBS)†*	14.9
	'Barbara Mandrell" (NBC)*	14.9
68.	"Flamingo Road" (NBC)*	14.8
69.	"CBS Tuesday Movie"	14.5
70.	"Simon & Simon" (CBS)	14.3
71.	"Best of the West" (ABC)*	13.9
72.	"ABC Friday Movie" (ABC)*	13.8
73.	"Bosom Buddies" (ABC)*	13.6
	"The Phoenix" (ABC)*	13.6
	"Strike Force" (ABC)*	13.6
76.	"No Soap, Radio" (ABC)†*	13.4
	"NBC Tuesday Movie"*	13.4
78.	"Harper Valley" (NBC)*	13.3
79.	"King's Crossing" (ABC)*	13.2
	'Jessica Novak" (CBS)†*	13.2
81.	"Code Red" (ABC)*	12.8
82.	"Nashville Palace (NBC)*	12.7
83.	"One of the Boys" (NBC)*	12.5
84.	"Maggie" (ABC)†*	12.3

†Five airings or fewer.
*Canceled.

RANK	SERIES	RATING
85.	"McClain's Law" (NBC)*	12.1
86.	"Darkroom" (ABC)*	11.7
	"Peacock Showcase" (NBC)†*	11.7
88.	"Making a Living" (ABC)*	11.5
89.	"Here's Boomer" (NBC)*	11.4
	"Shape of Things" (NBC)†*	11.4
91.	"Open All Night" (ABC)	11.2
92.	"Baker's Dozen" (CBS)†*	11.1
	"Cassie and Co." (NBC)†*	11.1
94.	"NBC Magazine"*	10.7
95.	"Lewis and Clark" (NBC)†*	10.5
96.	"Flintstones" (NBC)†*	10.4
97.	"Shannon" (CBS)*	10.3
98.	"Television: Inside and Out" (NBC)†*	10.1
	"Q.E.D." (CBS)†*	10.1
	"NBC Friday Movie"*	10.1
101.	"Chicago Story" (NBC)*	9.6
102.	"Billy Crystal Comedy Hour" (NBC)†*	9.5
103.	"Inside America" (ABC)†*	9.1
104.	"NBC Saturday Movie"*	8.8
105.	"Fitz and Bones" (NBC)†*	8.7

†Five airings or fewer.
*Canceled.

Epilogue

It was a beautiful spring day in Washington, D.C. The Rose Garden was the perfect spot for the President of the United States to make his announcement. Much to the pleasure of his constituency, Ronald Reagan was declaring a crusade to get prayer back into the public school system, even if it took another constitutional amendment to do it. On the evening news, Reagan looked strong, regal, self-assured—positively divine.

Standing next to him, smiling, smug, and equally divine was the Reverend Jerry Falwell, there to give the administration all the moral support it needed.

ABOUT THE AUTHOR

Marc Eliot graduated from Manhattan's High School of Performing Arts, received a B.A. degree from the City University of New York at City College, and an M.F.A. degree in the Writing Division of Columbia University's School of the Arts.

His previous books include *Death of a Rebel,* a biography of Phil Ochs; *American Television;* and *Burt!,* a biography of Burt Reynolds. In addition, Marc Eliot has written a prime-time special for NBC and was one of the producers of "The Tomorrow Show Coast-to-Coast." A frequent traveler, Marc Eliot lives in New York City and in Palenville, New York.